T0383423

Naked Architecture

*...to all the nudities with which
I have had dealings*

Valerio Paolo Mosco

Naked Architecture

Cover
Cecil Balmond
Weave Bridge
Steven Holl Architects
Busan Cinema Complex
Bak Arquitectos
Casa JD Vivienda de Veraneo
Valerio Olgiati
Perm Museum XXI
Patkau Architects
Our Lady of the Assumption
Parish Church
José María Sánchez García
Sports Centre
BIG – Bjarke Ingels Group
National Gallery of Greenland

Back Cover
Louis I. Kahn
with Anne Tyng
Project for the Philadelphia
City Hall Tower

First published in Italy in 2012
by Skira Editore S.p.A.
Palazzo Casati Stampa
via Torino 61
20123 Milano
Italy
www.skira.net

Art Director
Marcello Francone

Editor
Luca Molinari

Editorial Coordination
Vincenza Russo

Editing
Marina Marcello

Layout
Paola Ranzini

Iconographical Research
Paola Lamanna

Translations
Lucian Comoy
and Christopher Evans
for Language Consulting
Congressi, Milan

Printed and bound in Italy.
First edition

ISBN: 978-88-572-0472-7
Distributed in USA, Canada,
Central & South America by
Rizzoli International
Publications, Inc., 300 Park
Avenue South, New York, NY
10010, USA.
Distributed elsewhere in the
world by Thames and Hudson
Ltd., 181A High Holborn,
London WC1V 7QX, United
Kingdom.

Acknowledgments
This book owes much
to the assistance of Lorena
Di Girolamo and all my friends
with whom I have thrashed
out the idea of naked
architecture.
Thanks in particular
go to Iolanda Vitale and Gianni
Chesti of the library of the
Architecture and Design
faculty of "La Sapienza"
University of Rome.

Contents

Foreword
Harry Francis Mallgrave

Valerio Paolo Mosco thinks very differently than I do. If I had a year to pon-
der a title for a book, ten years for that matter, I don't think I could have
come up with the appellation *Naked Architecture*. Yet in glancing through
his images, essays, and such delineatory categories as "thin" or "primitive" architecture, I must say it works. It works rather well, in fact, because of the numerous, often stunning images that are assembled. It works
because of the seriousness with which he frames his historical argument.
It works because of the wealth of creative talents within the culture of glob-
al architecture today. It works because he touches upon something of great
importance for understanding and experiencing architecture – which I
will return to momentarily.

The story of modern architecture undressing itself over the last century or two has been told in a variety of ways, as Mosco relates. Architecture, if we take it back to its roots in evolutionary time – say 50,000 years
ago – was probably born of curiosity, wonder, pattern-making, and mys-
tery. It formed around a mythology of ceremonies and rituals in service to
fertility, puberty, good hunting, and the afterlife. It grew out of tribal cus-
toms, chanting, dance, and shamanism. If Le Corbusier would occasion-
ally paint in the nude, I have no doubt that more than a few therianthropes
did the same as they were first experimenting with red hematite on cave
walls. As for the dress codes of the day, nudity was undoubtedly the norm,
at least during the warmer seasons and during the hunt. Yet when tribal
sorcerers were moved to plead with the gods for a rain storm or the appearance of a herd, they more than likely did dress up, if only with animal heads, beads, and body paint. And because the first social essays in
built environments were probably to house the deities, we can assume that
they too were formed and dressed with symbols and patterns. Semper was
therefore probably correct in asserting that textiles grew out of mat-mak-
ing, and that those alabaster panels with which the Assyrian despots
adorned their palace walls were stylized after earlier carpets. The architectural dressing was not only polite but also expressive of an emerging
civilization that, with growing wealth, aspired to showcase its accomplish-
ments. Dressing became the norm for all world cultures over much of
recorded history. No 19th-century architect could have conceived of designing
a ritualized place for theater or opera and leaving it undressed. It would
lack ceremony and not stand up to personal decor.

The modernism of the early 20th century, as we know, changed this
course of things and it did so for a variety of reasons. The transfer of wealth
to a growing middle class simply did not leave enough money to go around,
and the destruction of wealth through economic depressions and world wars

Le Corbusier in front
of his mural painting,
villa E1027,
Roquebrune-Cap-Martin

greatly exacerbated the problem. And the result – the new bare architecture of concrete, steel, and glass – was not always that pleasing. The public, as J. M. Richards pointed out in 1940, generally disliked the new materials and its underlying aesthetic, and following the ensuing Holocaust even some of the champions of the new nudity, such as Giedion and Zevi, were forced to admit that something was wrong. To cut a long story short, CIAM with its faulty premises collapsed by the end of the fifties, and later stylistic permutations intended to solve the problem with a new symbolic dress – postmodernism and deconstruction – often changed a bad situation to a worse one. We are lucky to have survived the century at all.

The nineties has since brought along a number of things, good and bad. In the first category, it gave us a primer in environmental thinking; it gave us a new appreciation of tectonic culture; it gave us a simpler and less intellectualized use of form. It introduced as well a few things that we need not discuss, such as diagrammatic architecture, iconic architecture, virtual architecture, and digitalism in general. It also signaled, as Mosco correctly notes, the beginning of a more tactile architecture, a return to naked materiality. To this list I would add one more thing, which I regard as one of the many monumental discoveries of the nineties, a discovery that also explains what was missing from much of 20th-century modernism.

The discovery took place in a laboratory in Parma, in fact, and it was made by a team of Italian scientists led by Giacomo Rizzolatti. They were placing electrodes in the neocortices of macaque brains in search of patterns involved with such motor acts as eating a piece of fruit. They found these patterns but they also found something quite unexpected. Not only did a specific patch of neurons fire when the monkeys instigated certain movements but the same group of neurons also fired in monkeys who were simply watching other monkeys perform the acts. In short, they found that the monkeys were simulating the motor activities of other monkeys and they called these groups of nerve cells "mirror neurons". As these experiments were transferred to humans with the aid of the new neuroimaging technologies, the scientists came to a grander realization that we are born with and develop certain neurological templates that fire in response to the events of the world. We not only mentally simulate the actions and intentions of others but also their emotions, as well as – as we have more recently learned – the qualities of inanimate objects, among them our interface with the built environment. Vittorio Gallese, who was one of the scientists involved with the discovery, has called this mimetic power "embodied simulation", and its growing sophistication seems to explain a lot of things: the burst of artistic culture around 50,000 years ago, our language and frequent use of metaphors, our intersubjectivity, our capacity to learn, why the twisted columns in the courtyard of St. John Lateran induces tension in our bodies, and indeed how those early therianthropes learned to paint so well.

To this discovery soon came another, again by a team of Italian scientists, which demonstrated that when the visual cortex of the occipital lobe is involved with perceiving an object, it sets off a much larger circuit of active neurons in the somatosensory cortex, the prefrontal cortex, and in the anterior cingulate cortex. What this means is that every wall we see we also feel in the tactile area of the brain, as if we were rubbing our hands along its surface; every object we see also lights up the hedonic and emotional centers of the brain, for better or worse.

These discoveries, I believe, explain much of the appeal of naked architecture, especially when it possesses high sensory effects or what Zumthor calls the condition of being "real". They explain in part why modern architecture, with its black-and-white glass boxes, was so often ridiculed for producing "cold and monotonous" forms.

These discoveries also prove that Descartes was pretty much wrong in believing that thinking was a mental activity. We are preeminently and primordially sensory creatures. As emotional organisms, we crave environmental stimulation and respond immediately – somatically and viscerally – with our bodies. We simulate lifting the boulders in Smiljan Radic's restaurant; we gravitate toward the beams of sunlight in Nishizawa's museum; we celebrate the sound of our feet on the boards of a tea house in Portugal; we are filled with glowing warmth in approaching the Patkaus' church in Vancouver. I am not saying that all architecture should exalt sensory effects. But I will say that architects should consider a little more carefully the basics of how we experience a built environment, which I would argue is in a far less conceptualized manner than often supposed. Biologically, we could use a little more naked architecture, but this time let's return these naked bodies to a luscious Garden of Eden!

Naked Architecture
Valerio Paolo Mosco

"Nudity presupposes the absence of clothes, but it is not the same thing [...]. Nudity is something that one notices whereas the absence of clothes is something that passes unobserved".
Giorgio Agamben

The Return of Nudity

Recently we have been seeing the return to a naked architecture in many places: architecture that is stripped bare, wiped clean, anti-decorative, simplified not just in its forms, but also in its conceptual machinery. It is a generalized phenomenon, from the bottom up, that makes no reference to a defined system of thought, has no putative fathers and is not supported by any academic institution. What is certain is that the return to nudity (for nudity in architecture is never an invention, but always a return) represents a significant break with a past that has seen the proliferation of works of architecture of quite another kind: dressed up, tending to conceal their bodies as much as possible. Frank O. Gehry's well-known Guggenheim Museum in Bilbao (opened in 1997) can be considered the epigone of an architectural season beginning in the sixties that has exalted facing to the point of making it first an icon in its own right, and then a sculpture enveloping the whole body of the building. This kind of architecture, aptly defined as the "architecture of envelopes", has for several decades represented a paradigm of reference in that it was supposed to allow expression of the highest degree of iconographic and plastic freedom, making possible the fulfilment of that desire for communication at all costs typical of the postmodernism. But over time this freedom has turned first into mannerism, and then licence and in some cases caprice, so that the envelopes have come to reveal their limitations, made even more evident by a precocious aging of their facings, which have rapidly lost their initial glittering perfection. The current rediscovery of nudity in architecture should be regarded in the first place as a reaction against the architecture of envelopes, a phenomenon that not coincidentally is emerging at a moment in history in which the aggressive capitalism of early globalization, of which these envelopes represented the monumental expression, seems to be imploding in a deep crisis whose traits are not yet clearly defined, but are undoubtedly structural and as such not of brief duration.

Today's naked architecture presents itself in extremely diverse forms. Naked are those works of architecture that seek to turn the structure into images of the building; naked are those works of architecture whose surfaces are not decorated, perhaps treated with fluidity or plastic dynamism, but in any case bare. Necessarily naked as well are works of architecture for the so-called developing countries or for the Third World, in a certain sense obliged to be bare, as too are those that intend to create the impression of humble frugality, in line with today's prevailing paradigm of sustainability. The panorama of nudity is therefore extremely varied and trying to lump it together by means of precise formal categories, of pure visibility, is not

Masaccio
Expulsion of Adam and Eve from the Garden of Eden,
1424–28
Florence, Brancacci Chapel

only a difficult undertaking, but also debases the result of an architectural expression whose meaning extends beyond its formal connotations into a controversial, essentially symbolic and certainly enigmatic territory.[1] In fact the sensation that one gets when dealing with nudity, not just in architecture but also in philosophy and art, as Giorgio Agamben has shown,[2] is that of a tangible obviousness, easily perceptible and yet elusive, as if nudity were an oil so essential as to evaporate as soon as it comes into contact with the air. One fact remains clear: in the return to nakedness architecture (as often happens) lags behind the other arts, which have long rediscovered the figurative value of the body and, by this rediscovery, freed themselves of the now sterile vestiges of abstract modernism, an operation which architecture has yet to complete. In art this rediscovery passed through Marcel Duchamp. A century ago Apollinaire declared that Duchamp was the only modern painter to take a real interest in the nude. As Octavio Paz explained in his masterly study of Duchamp, with the significant title *Appearance Stripped Bare*, Duchamp replaced the iconological nude (the nude as theme of representation), with a symbolic nude and as such one that laid bare metaphysical essences.[3] An interpretation that has taken on new life today, radicalized and manipulated in the work of artists like Matthew Barney, Vanessa Beecroft, Marina Abramovich and many others.[4]

The aim of this work is not just to point out a tendency in contemporary architecture, but more in general to recount, from the perspective of the past, a paradigm that for over two hundred years has corresponded to the innermost motivations of the Modern, but whose enigmatic implications mean that it remains elusive.

Nudity as Metaphor, as Myth and as Degree Zero

It is necessary to start out from a significant contradiction: the nudity of bodies cannot be related directly to architecture. A body is in fact naked when it uncovers its skin; a work of architecture on the other hand is not "actually" naked, but "appears" so when its covering, i.e. its skin, is removed, or reduced to a minimum. A concept that is moreover underlined in ordinary language when a skeleton in reinforced concrete or steel is said to be bare even though a skeleton does not correspond exactly to the body; if anything it is what is left after its death. Nudity in architecture is a metaphor, a rhetorical expression that does not identify with precision the thing itself, but describes it through a figure of speech that can easily be grasped and communicated. In other words nudity is something like what Kant might have considered it to be: a representation of the imagination, capable of defining not so much an aspect as a characteristic. So it is no accident that it was perceived for the first time in the 18th century, after Kant, when aesthetics broke away definitively from ethics and tradition. This transcendence of appearances took place for nudity via two modalities: one which we might define as immanent and Romantic, another as transcendent and metaphysical. Let us begin with the first by making a statement of fact. Nudity is not achieved completely in buildings that are in use, but is expressed fully only at two extreme moments of their existence: when they are under construction and when they fall into ruin. Nakedness cor-

Friedrich Gilly
Project for a mausoleum,
c. 1798

responds therefore to the alpha and the omega of any work of architecture. It marks its inevitable beginning as well as its inevitable end and in so doing links two Romantic myths: that of the futurist "city that rises" (the form under construction, the *Werkform*) and that of Piranesi's "speaking ruins" (the form in ruin, the *Ruinform*).[5] By making the construction and the ruin react with one another, nudity presages that *Urform*, that primary, archetypal and necessary form which has been sought in different ways by great Romantic authors like Goethe, Herder, von Humboldt and Burckhardt, and from another perspective by Baudelaire.[6] The other degree of nudity, the transcendent one, has its roots in mythology. In his book with the telling title *The Architecture of Good Intentions*, Colin Rowe, with that ironic grace the English possess when they deal with overarching systems, rewrites the Biblical myth of the expulsion of Adam and Eve from the Garden of Eden in order to capture the essence of the modern spirit in architecture.[7] As is well-known, as soon as they were driven out of Paradise our progenitors discovered their nakedness and the awareness of their now shameful state is represented by the shaky fig leaf they are obliged to wear. Thus the leaf, as well as being humanity's first item of clothing, is also the symbol of a disastrous event from which the human race is descended. Rowe adds that apparently nothing would prevent Adam and Eve from getting rid of the fig leaf, repenting and trying to get back into Eden, perhaps by a back door where they might find an indulgent St Peter or Karl Marx. For Rowe this is the "good intention" that is at the root of the Modern: a symbolic stripping naked by which it might be possible to return to a Paradise that has not necessarily been lost forever.[8] For Rowe therefore, as in a different way for Giedion and Sedlmayr, in its desire for metaphysical purity, nudity corresponds to the stigmata of modernity, to the initiatory wounds without which the very concept of modern architecture would lose its *raison d'être*.[9]

All this is with regard to "chief systems", in Galileo's words; in more pragmatic terms, on the other hand, there is a way in which nudity can appear more tangible. In 1981 Bruno Zevi, referring to Roland Barthes from whom he borrowed the concept, wrote: "[...] the 'degree zero' is a familiar notion in the history of art [...] it can be called primitivism, dissolution of grammatical or syntactic systems, disintegration of a code [...]. [The degree zero] is a recurrent phenomenon in certain periods, when formalism prevails and linguistic dogmas rule out a true evolution, at times in which an urgent need is felt to regain the semantic specificity of words to combat the bad habit of hand-me-down phrases: the "degree zero" offers a means of infusing new blood and vitality into an exhausted language".[10] From Zevi's words we can infer a correspondence between nudity and the degree zero: both are, as Giambattista Vico would have put it, cyclical reactions, therapeutic and inevitable "dynamic phenomena of regeneration" whose task is to set at zero what is in decline but out of inertia tiredly carries on. Zevi offers the example of the Romanesque: the bare, essential, even shaky walls of the Romanesque, in the light of the degree zero, are interpreted as an inevitable reaction to Byzantine architecture, to its affected filigree decoration, no longer relevant in a world that had discovered other values and a different vision of the world. Zevi goes even further; for him the degree zero does not find expression solely as a figurative reaction, but is also the symptom of a more general reaction against theoretical constructions that aim to legitimate architectonic forms through intellectual constructions. In *As You Like It*, William Shakespeare provides a vivid description of these constructions, calling them "sermons in stone": pedantic homilies that build up continually until they eventually collapse under their own weight. Viewed from the perspective of the notion of degree zero, Shakespeare's phrase refers to our own day. The last few decades have seen the proliferation of masses of ever more complex sermons in stone, almost all starting out from the structuralist argument that a building is comparable to a text that can be read in almost endless ways. If on the one hand this has permitted an ever more refined richness of interpretation, on the other it has driven the debate into an increasingly redundant hall of mirrors where, in the infinite refractions between words and things, common sense has been lost and sometimes even good sense. The long chain that runs all the way from historicism through conceptual architecture, deconstructivism, and blob design to irrelevant works of immaterial and digital architecture demonstrates today the vanity of too many sermons with ever scantier results. In the face of all this the reaction takes the form of a desire to start over, to return to a degree zero that will bring architecture back to tangible if not figurative values, laying it bare not only physically but also conceptually. A desire for a return to zero that can be summed up by Nietzsche's Zarathustra, who in honour of a vitalism unconditioned by the intellect, declares: "Body am I entirely, and nothing else".[11]

Giovanni Battista Piranesi
Rovine di villa Adriana,
c. 1770

The Disputed Nudity of the Primitive Hut
The image that even today encapsulates the degree zero in architecture with the greatest efficacy is the frontispiece of Abbé Laugier's treatise illustrating the well-known primitive hut (1753). It shows the muse of architecture seated dejectedly on what look like the ruins of an ornate rococo building. A boy, symbolizing the architecture that is to come, indicates the future to the muse, which corresponds to a rustic primitive hut of interwoven branches: the most naked architecture that can be imagined, constructed (evidently on the instructions of Rousseau) by a noble savage with the sincere force of an unspoiled state of nature.[12] This image, which quickly became an icon, ignited a debate that is at the root of the Modern. We will briefly summarize its main passages.[13] In 1768 Milizia, drawing upon the lesson of Lodoli, proposed nine principles upon which to refound the discipline. Among these, the fourth declares that architecture, being the child of necessity, has to make sure that each of its elements appears necessary, and so "everything done for mere ornament is a defect".[14] This precept, which amounts to one of the first expressions of the modern degree zero, delegitimizes the ancient one of the imitation of nature and with it the system of orders and ornamentation. All this in the name of a new thesis: functional essentiality, that as such can only be expressed through nudity. A few decades after Milizia, the architects of the Enlightenment, Boullée, Ledoux and Lequeu, translated the new spirit of the time into an architecture of naked volumes that expressed an eloquent monumentality so out of scale as to infuse a

Marc-Antoine Laugier
Essai sur l'Architecture
Title-page of the 1755
edition

terrifying sense of dismay. In them decoration became no more than a fragment, an *appliqué* on shamelessly bare architecture.[15] And it was precisely with the Enlightenment architects that nudity had one of its first trans-
figurations: born with theorists like Laugier and Milizia as a moral precept
legitimized by anthropology, it was transformed into an aesthetic expression capable of translating into forms that feeling of the sublime of which
Burke and Kant had spoken.

In the early decades of the 19th century a further transfiguration took
place, this time brought about by Heinrich Hübsch who in 1828 declared
that the new architecture would have to be based on the structural skeleton as an objective moulding principle and as such an expression of authentic
beauty, an idea that would be taken up after him by Karl Friedrich Schinkel.[16]
Thus nudity, which up until that moment had found expression with the
abolition of decoration, sought an alternative mode of expression, one that
would no longer be on the surface, but enter the body of the architecture
through its structure, and this a few years before Paxton built the Crystal
Palace (1851) and Labrouste the interior of the Reading Room of the Bib-
liothèque Sainte Geneviève (1842–50), the first works of architecture in
which nudity and structure coincide. The hypothesis of a naked structural
beauty became a *fait accompli* in the second half of the 19th century. In
1881 it was Leopold Eidlitz who in the name of empathy theory, very popular at the time, spoke explicitly of the "feeling of structure" as an evident
sign of beauty,[17] a principle that with Eugène Viollet-le-Duc gave rise to a
now definitively systematized philosophy, able to find expression in a style.
What interested Viollet-le-Duc was the definition of a new form, one that
starting out from an analytical analysis of the structural elements, suitably
divided between supporting and supported ones, would define a system in
which the static function is clearly revealed. To achieve this it was necessary for the individual elements to renounce any plastic attribute apart
from the structural one, through an operation of denudation.[18] Viollet-le-
Duc's radical ideas would be followed through by Auguste Choisy and by Ana-
tole de Baudot, designer of the first naked interior in reinforced concrete:
the church of Saint-Jean-de-Montmartre in Paris (1894–1904).

Up to this point the justifications of what we might define as "pure"
naked architecture, the one starting from Laugier and following an analytical and reductionist course, were used to make explicit what was po-
tentially already present in Milizia's ideas: i.e. that the naked structure corresponded to the highest meaning of architecture. In parallel to this radical interpretation more complex ideas were developed. In 1852 Gottfried
Semper questioned the idea of Laugier's primitive hut, considered less
than plausible from an anthropological point of view.[19] The hypothesis that
our ancestors would have lived in a hut with no covering, and therefore no
protection from inclement weather, appeared unlikely to Semper. In the
light of this obvious fact he proposed an alternative: a more carefully reasoned Caribbean hut made up of four elements: base, hearth, structure
and light framework of covering for the roof and walls.[20] So Semper
"clothed" Laugier's hut of pure structure by proposing a distinction between
a solid structural core anchored to the ground and a light woven enclo-

sure: to the first is entrusted the statics of the building, to the second its representative aspects.[21] As Harry Mallgrave and after him Kenneth Frampton have pointed out, Semper gave no precedence to either of the two components, thereby laying the foundations for a confrontation (if not a conflict), between the considerations of the structure, as expression of an ethical foundation, and those of the facing, as expression instead of the needs of communication: a conflict that persists to our own day.[22]

Essential Years for Naked Architecture

Yet another transfiguration of nudity came at the end of the 19th century. In 1878 Konrad Fiedler contradicted Semper and, calling for a return to a radical model along Laugier's lines, proposed the removal of the covering again. But when Fiedler eliminated that covering (and this is the new element), he did not lay bare a skeletal trilithic structure, but ancestral, essential walls, devoid of ornament.[23] So by the end of the 19th century the dual nature of nudity was clear: on the one hand skeletal structural nudity, which found its model in steel-and-glass constructions, on the other that of the wall, which had been prognosticated by the architects of the Enlightenment.[24] Within a short space of time this dialectical relationship extended to disclose new concepts. In 1893 August Schmarsow, starting from Fiedler's axiom that the wall is the generative element of architecture, was the first to free himself from the anthropology that had held the debate to ransom up to then. Thus he proposed the wall not as an end but as a means of grasping what Schmarsow himself considered the primary essence of architecture, i.e. space: a quality that appeared for the first time as a consequence of the denudation of the walls, as was to happen for the first time in the theatrical scenery designed by Adolphe Appia a few years later.

The result of this broadening of perspective generated what we might call "the triangle of Modern", at whose vertices we find the structure, the facing and the new-born space; in the middle, floating between the vertices, nudity.

This triangle was to define the limits within which the so-called proto-rationalist architects would move.[25] First of all Hendrik Petrus Berlage who at the turn of the century designed the Amsterdam Stock Exchange (1896–1903) a building that, as Sigfried Giedion and after him Mies van der Rohe declared, had the value of an apparition able to "purify architecture".[26] The Stock Exchange arose from several observations: the first was that steel-and-glass structures, although necessary, had no architectural dignity, and therefore needed to be combined with the brick wall. To find a synthesis between the two technologies it was necessary to strip down the wall as much as possible, making it a "shaven wall", in other words to bring it to a certain degree of dematerialization that would allow it to be wedded to the iron structure, as in fact happens in the Stock Exchange. This aspiration became for Berlage a programme at whose root nudity was set: "One can speak of a work of architecture only when what predominates is the logical-constructive principle of the facing which is not an inconsistent envelope that denies the structure nor a dressing, but is indissolubly linked to the internal construction [...]. Therefore it is necessary

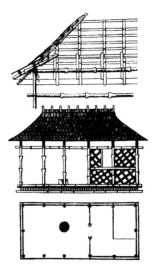

Gottfried Semper
Scheme of the
Caribbean hut,
from *Der Stil*, 1851

to study first of all the skeleton, i.e. the naked construction in all its vigour, in order to grasp the body in its entirety, without confusing it with the clothing. So even the last veil, the fig leaf, must fall, for the truth we want is completely naked. Architecture was a person dressed in the worst fashion [...] and so the fashionable garment has to be eliminated to bring out the form without wrapping, i.e. its nature, its truth".[27]

In the same period in which Berlage wrote this, Frank Lloyd Wright built the Unity Temple in Oak Park, Chicago, the first building constructed out of reinforced concrete poured on site and not clad: a revolutionary object in that it seemed to resolve, through a new technology, the now open conflict between structure and facing. Berlage declared at a lecture in 1905, the same year as the opening of Wright's building: "[poured reinforced concrete] corresponds to the legitimate aspiration to the style and culture that are to come, which is that of the undecorated object, of the unadorned building, of the inherent beauty of the material".[28] Thus the concrete has to appear naked, to demonstrate its nature as a material without connections and joints. To these precepts Berlage admitted only two liberties, which were to have extreme importance after the Second World War with Le Corbusier and Brutalism: painting and the rough texture given to poured surfaces by the formwork.

In general the years between 1890 and 1910 were crucial with regard to nudity and the questions related to it, in particular the elimination of decoration and the relationship between structure and envelope.

Among cultivated Viennese architects it was facing that prevailed. Otto Wagner was the first to prophesy that the new architecture, which he explicitly defined as "modern", would tend to have flat surfaces and use materials in their natural state.[29] Out of these premises he developed a basically spare but not naked architecture, faced with applied surfaces that had almost no thickness, as if they were sheets of cloth.[30] His pupils, Joseph Hoffmann and Joseph Maria Olbrich, with the exception of two explicitly nude works (the Purkersdorf Sanatorium in Vienna of 1906 and the

Exhibition Building at the Darmstadt Artists' Colony of 1904), would take Wagner's position centred on the representative and communicative power of the facing.[31] It was Adolf Loos, in an important essay of 1898, who gave a theoretical underpinning to Wagner's premises, proposing a genuine philosophy of facing based on two precepts: that wall and facing should never be muddled up and that the facing itself ought not to have decorations of any kind. The corollary of the theory of facing was space, and this meant following what today we might consider a sophism, the idea that the prime effect of the art of facing is the delimitation of a space.[32]

On the figure of Loos the words of Renato De Fusco are telling: "The simplification of the forms, their emancipation from the decorative spirit typical of the Sezession and the followers of Art Nouveau, constitutes in the first place a choice of essential configurations that are valid precisely for the taste, the tendency, the decision to go for simplicity. This translates into a struggle against waste and the superfluous, taking on in addition a moral accent and a precise social connotation, but what drives this radical aristocratic architect is in the first place, as has been said, an aesthetic choice".[33]

Antonio Sant'Elia
Study of Terraced
Building, 1913

While in Vienna the choice seemed in favour of cladding, in France, following a tradition ushered in by Laugier and carried further by Viollet-le-Duc, it was structure that prevailed. The whole of Auguste Perret's research, fundamental to the theoretical development of the reinforced-concrete structure, was based on Viollet-le-Duc's argument that "if the structure is not worthy of remaining in view, the architect has misunderstood his mission. The facing and filling materials should complete the framework, but without diminishing it: it is necessary to show a beam where there is a beam and a pillar where there is a pillar".[34]

What interested Perret was the quest for an ideal relationship between framework and filling. The result was works which had a twofold significance: on the one hand they freed the architecture of structure from Neo-Gothic tendencies, decanting it into a now pacified classical form, while on the other they laid the foundations for the rigorous reductionism to which Le Corbusier would make explicit reference. Less tied to the building and more urban was the interpretation of Tony Garnier, who regarded the nudity of exposed concrete as the infrastructure on which to develop another language. In the report on his utopian project of the Citè Industrielle Garnier wrote: "[...] Let us note, moreover, that if our structure stays simple, without ornament, without mouldings, bare everywhere, we can then add decorative arts, in all their forms".[35]

Architectonic nudity and its implications were therefore the basis of architectural debate preceding the First World War, with a theoretical clarity even more noteworthy now than it was then. Nevertheless, unnoticed by the proto-rationalist architects, nude architecture was already being constructed spontaneously and on a grand scale. Sant'Elia was first to take note, seeing in anonymous industrial constructions (such as factories, warehouses and granaries) images of a majestic new style: a naked, functional attitude which is to replace bourgeois decorativism into cities.[36] Immediatly after the war, following this futuristic intuition, Poelzig, Gropius,

Photo of silos on the Buffalo River, from Reyner Banham, *A Concrete Atlantis: U.S. Industrial Building and European Modern Architecture 1900–1925*, 1986

Mendelsohn and Le Corbusier created a genuine industrial mania. Photographs of American works of industrial architecture (retouched more often than not to appear even more naked) seemed to be models so complete as to indicate the way of the new style finally appropriated to the civilization of machines. The road seemed clear, and yet within a short period of time modern architecture took another direction. The critic Reyner Banham was one of the few to notice this shift. He wrote: "One can see building up [...] an incipient school of factory designers [...] eschewing decoration and handling sculptural forms with great boldness, a boldness to be matched only in Futurist projects at that time. Immediately after the War it looked as if this school could resume where it had broken off [...]. But the movement was quickly inhibited by the Dutch and Russian Abstract aesthetics mentioned above, and came to nothing".[37] Banham's statement is extremely interesting in so far as it underlines the fact that the immediate, sensorial and romantic nudity, that had always been appealing since Laugier until the Futurists, was set aside by the avant-gardes, which focused instead on the construction of new languages and the definition with them of new principles and rules. So by the twenties industrial nudity was sidelined by avant-gardes: an attempt to substitute it by abstraction and composition. An experiment whose limitations would be grasped by Le Corbusier and Mies van der Rohe, who would be very careful not to get caught in the quicksand of a language made an end in itself by loosing the figurative and symbolic substance.

White and Grey Nudity in Le Corbusier

Le Corbusier can be considered a diviner of the naked form, having interpreted it in almost all its aspects, always in reference to Quatremère de Quincy's view that the primary forms of architecture could not be derived solely from the rustic hut, but also from caves and tents. He gave one of his first houses, Villa Schwob at La Chaux-de-Fonds (1916), an explicitly unadorned façade that Rowe interprets as a manneristic expression, but which it would be more logical to consider the prelude to Purist nudity.[38] With the Maison Domino (1914), Le Corbusier presented the first mature interpretation of nudity. The Maison, which owes a great deal to Perret and his pared-down classicism, can be seen as the translation of Laugier's hut into reinforced concrete. The idea was to provide a rough skeleton to be clad with an envelope capable of relating directly to the structural core. As is well-known, the solution he found was to hang on the skeleton (which has pillars set back from the surfaces of the façade) thin non-structural walls treated as if they were blank sheets of white paper on which to freely set out the system of openings. Thus Le Corbusier resolved the question of the relationship between structural core and facing raised by Semper by contrasting the two entities drastically: on the one hand the crude skeletal core, which we could define as Dionysian, on the other the polished and Apollonian facing. As Charles Jenks has fittingly pointed out, this way of proceeding by dialectical opposites is characteristic of Le Corbusier's entire activity, influencing not only his choices, but his disposition as well.[39] A few years after the Maison Domino, Le Corbusier proposed with the Maison Cit-

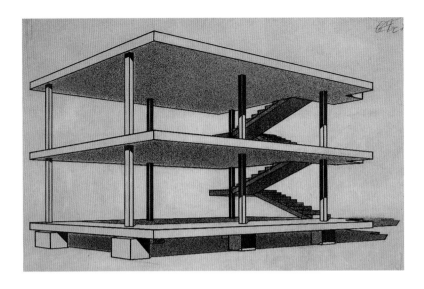

rohan (1920) an alternative nudity, one that replaced the skeleton in reinforced concrete with white plastered walls. This is how the architect described the work: "Simplification of the light sources; a single large window at either end, two supporting side walls; a flat roof above; a genuine box that could be used as a house".[40] Thus skeleton and box, both of them bare, define the poles between which a line of research was organized by continual hybridizations, a research that found paradigmatic expression in the Purist villas of the twenties, summed up by Le Corbusier himself in a sketch that bears witness to his astonishing capacity for conceptual synthesis.

However, as well as being an architect, Le Corbusier was a painter. For him it was in meaningful forms that lurked the spirit of the times which an artist had the duty to pursue in order to translate it into language. The aim of his famous book *Vers une architecture* (1923) was thus to establish the characteristics of the Modernist iconography of the civilization of the machines.[41] To achieve this he compiled a varied and diverse list of objects, including transatlantic liners, aeroplanes, iron bridges and large and anonymous American silos (which had already attracted the attention first of Hermann Muthesius and then Walter Gropius and Erich Mendelsohn), to which

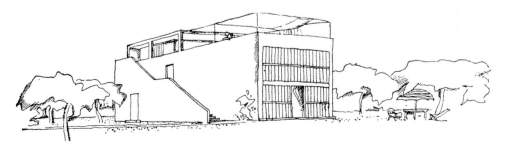

he added the ruins of works of architecture of the past, first of all the Parthenon. What unites this heterogeneous list, allowing it also to be seen as a homogeneous corpus, is an unadorned essentiality capable of inspiring a bare, intrinsic and immediate necessity, when all is said and done not very distant from the one prophesied by the empirical philosophers in the 18th century. Thus, at the beginning of the thirties, Le Corbusier came up with such a clear interpretation of nudity that it became the foundation of the International Style presented to the world in 1932 by Henry-Russel Hitchcock and Philip Johnson in the famous exhibition at the MoMA in New York.[42] But at the very moment of its consecration Le Corbusier changed course and discovered a nudity of quite another kind: rough, crude, even rustic. The sense of this new direction was expressed by the architect himself when, referring to his 1935 project for the Weekend House, he declared that he had wanted to design a dwelling that would express an "essential attitude" by which all that would be seen would correspond to the elements of anonymous and popular constructions.[43] This hypothesis would be systematized five years later, in 1940, with the frugal and Mediterranean Maisons Murondins. Thus in the space of twenty years Le Corbusier "invented" two kinds of nudity: the first, from the top down, was Purist and abstract and as such could be defined as "white"; the other instead was from the bottom up, popular and vernacular, and as such could be called "grey". This dual nudity did not pertain to Le Corbusier alone: for example Gropius (with Adolf Meier), shortly before designing some of the icons of white rationalism like the Herald Tribune skyscraper or the Bauhaus, constructed the crude Sommerfeld House (1920): a totally anti-Purist building that Joseph Rykwert appropriately described as paradigmatic of the archaic and frugal spirit that runs covertly throughout the Modern.[44] And yet, despite the evidence of a dual spirit, the curators of the aforementioned exhibition on the *International Style* censored grey nudity for propagandistic reasons, as it undermined their theoretical construction. This ostracism persisted at least until the early fifties when the hypothesis of a return to low-cost construction became established as an anti-rhetorical expression aimed at regenerating the meaning of architecture from the bottom up after the trauma of the war. Italy, joined later by Britain and France, was the centre of this new trend. Even before the war Giuseppe Pagano had anticipated, with his photographic reportages on working-class housing in *Casabella*, the neorealism of the following decade, in which the dignity of

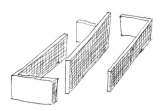
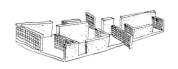

anonymous and bare rustic building was taken as a model for a hoped-for regeneration of the language, a thesis that as is well-known would be taken up by literature and especially cinema after the war.[45] The interest in humble and frugal architecture soon declined, but never disappeared completely and has remained present, but muted, until our own day, when we are seeing its enthusiastic revival on the tide of the paradigm of sustainability.

Always restless, Le Corbusier turned his back on this approach as well: in the fifties, just when frugal nudity was enjoying international success, he moved on once again from his discoveries and, starting out from what had already been hinted at in the Swiss Pavilion at the Cité Universitaire in Paris (1930–32), focused his attention upon cast on site and reinforced concrete left in a natural state of which Wright and Berlage had spoken years before. The idea was to shape a monolithic sculptural mass, capable of translating the ancestral expressive force of *art brut* into architecture. The buildings in Chandigarh (1952–65), like the later La Tourette Monastery (1957–60), became the expression of a new sculptural and austere style, in which Le Corbusier the architect, the sculptor and the painter all converged in a sort of personal naked work of total art.[46] The result was the invention of Brutalism (the term coined in 1955 by Alison and Peter Smithson[47]), which would regenerate the International Style through the rediscovery of the sculptural mass after years of predominance of the plane. Towards the end of his career Le Corbusier allowed himself to realize one of the most eloquent monuments of naked architecture: the Tower of Shadows in Chandigarh (1960), a genuine homage to the rustic skeleton and its Romantic capacity to inspire the epic melancholy of ruins or buildings under construction. Thus nudity in Le Corbusier, after a long journey, returned to its origins, to its primary inspiration.

The Ontology and Theology of Nudity: Mies and Schwarz

While for Le Corbusier nudity was an end, for Mies van der Rohe it was a means. Bare skeletons made a great impression on Mies in the early, Expressionist period of his career, prompting him to write: "Only skyscrapers under construction reveal their bold constructive thoughts, and then the impression made by their soaring skeletal frames is overwhelming. With the raising of the walls, this impression is completely destroyed: the constructive thought, the necessary basis for artistic form-giving, is annihilated and frequently smothered by a meaningless and trivial jumble of forms [...] one would have to give up the attempt to solve a new task with traditional forms; rather one should attempt to give form to the new task out of the nature of this task".[48] Mies, like Le Corbusier, was aware of the ambiguity between structure and cladding identified by Semper and he attempted to give a response to this ambiguity. The problem emerged clearly in the Friedrichstrasse Skyscraper Project (1919–21). In both the designs presented, in order to maintain an immediate sensation of skeletal nudity, the glass facing is treated like an intangible veil so as to obtain an effect of dematerialization that it was impossible to create with the technologies of the time. After these projects Mies laid aside the problem of cladding skeletons, only to take it up again twenty years later in the United States

where technology would provide him with the means he needed to solve it. In general the projects of the German period aimed at translating the new-born languages of the avant-gardes, above all Neo-Plasticism, into a constructively plausible architecture.[49] In view of this intention it is more logical to look at Mies's early period in the light of essentiality rather than nudity, even if a project like the one for the brick country house (1923) seems to lie somewhere between the two terms. If we consider the Barcelona Pavilion (1929), for example, it looks stark but not naked: the walls for example are cladded with natural stone (onyx and Tinos marble), translating into abstract language Wagner and Loos's Viennese theory of facing, while the structure, consisting of point-like supports, is only part of the composition and Mies even seems to have added it at a later stage. In the end what we are facing here is a work that chooses to refer to Semper, rather than Laugier. The difference between nudity and essentiality is subtle, but important. We have seen that Le Corbusier certainly did not lack essentiality, but his was an essentiality that always found expression in a naked form. Mies on the other hand programmatically set out to transcend external appearance as such. Following the principle of his friend the philosopher Romano Guardini, he was convinced that there is a moment of pure necessity that comes even before the decision about form and that it is necessary to refer to this.[50] This conviction, in some ways iconoclastic, explains Mies's amazing and at the same time cryptic declaration: "we refuse to recognize problems of form".

In his later period in the United States Mies became even more essential, further reducing the scope of his own action to steel-and-glass construction and doing so in the hope of coming up with an answer to Semper's question of the facing of the skeleton left open since the time of the Friedrichstrasse Skyscraper Project.[51] The solution was already apparent in the early fifties with the Lake Shore Drive Apartments in Chicago (1948–50) in which the cladding was given a skeletal structure of its own independent of the core. Colin Rowe, Arthur Drexler, Fritz Neumeyer, William H. Jordy and Kenneth Frampton have given masterly accounts of the traits of Mies's poetics in the American period, in which each project was added to the others in a logical concatenation of extreme rigour and lucidity.[52] All of these authors, some directly and some indirectly, agree on the fact that Mies was interested in finding a way to reconcile the conflict between structure and cladding via technology with the aim of defining once and for all the ontological bases of a definitively modern architecture.[53] The means adopted to attain this end was a continual visual subtraction of the mass of the building in the hypothesis that a reduction of the latter to its minimum components would reveal the solution. This process, apparently simple but with ever more complex implications, was brought to a conclusion in two works: the Crown Hall (1950–56) and the Convention Hall project (1953–54), both in Chicago, in which structure and cladding coincide on the surface of the façade in such a way as to completely free up the space inside, becoming the absolute protagonist of the work.

In general Mies's research lies beyond nudity, in a sense transcending it. For Mies in fact the triangle defined by structure, cladding and space

does not have nudity at its centre, implicitly considered an ephemeral form, but the definition of a series of lasting forms that, as Antonio Monestiroli puts it, become the expression of a sense of dignity so eloquent that rises to the spirit of modernity.[54] An ontology of construction therefore and one that distrusts iconography, in which nudity is a necessary but not sufficient condition.

An interpretation of nudity that goes beyond Mies's is offered by Rudolf Schwarz. Schwarz was also a disciple of Romano Guardini and, unlike Mies, thought and reasoned in images. Many of his works and reflections concerned church architecture and how this had to find an expression suited to the times.[55] The St Fronleichnam Church (1929–30) is a rare example of nudity that is at once lofty and featureless. The idea, clear as a revelation, is that of a series of walls which it would be more appropriate to call chaste than abstract, containing a space that seems to breathe life into Guardini's words: "[...] this is not emptiness, this is silence! And it is from the silence of these vast walls that the presage of the presence of God can flower".[56] A few years later Schwarz built another church in which he made the choice instead of a vernacular and frugal nudity, one in which the elements of construction are clearly exposed and the finishings are kept to a minimum. The little chapel of St Albert at Leversbach (1931–32) is built of stone walls plastered on the inside on which the rough wooden trusses of the roof are set. The chapel was not well received by the local population, as Schwarz recalled: "Someone like us saw space between the bare walls and, behind the unfinished and rough, the finished image. The people, however, always saw the naked, the rough, the unfinished".[57] After the war Schwarz persevered with his research into essential buildings, with a mystical impact, always constructed using simple and immediate techniques. Simplicity in fact for Schwarz was an indispensable value: as well as corresponding to theological nudity, it became a formal precept. The hypothesis was summed up by Schwarz himself in a conceptual scheme in

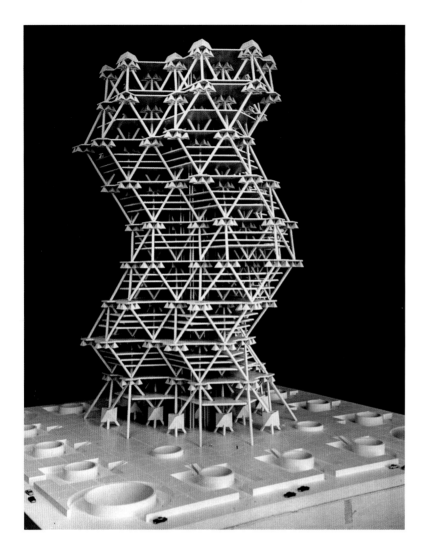

which a linear arabesque grows simpler at the top as if it were a Gothic building. At the bottom of the drawing Schwarz wrote: "the great construction of the layers of the hierarchical order gathers towards the top into ever simpler forms [...] everything grows clearer and more powerful as you move upwards".[58] Thus simplicity (a quality that lies somewhere between a corollary and a synonym of nudity) became in the thirties, with the passing of the stupefaction of the avant-gardes, the mark of modern architecture: it was interpreted in the light of the Romantic myth of the "great form", in Mies through ontology and in Schwarz through theology.[59] For them nudity and simplicity were raised to a conscious expression of the spirit, whereas for the majority of the architects of the Modern Movement they would be nothing but empty iconography elevated to propaganda.

Kahn and the Transfiguration of Naked Architecture

From the fifties onwards the idea of nudity lost its centrality for a variety of reasons. First of all the trauma caused by the Second World War, which made people yearn for a less dogmatic and more expressive architecture. Added to this was the aspiration to a greater complexity of architectural thought and form which meant that reductionism, one of the cornerstones of the Modern Movement, lost much of its allure. Architects sought less paradigmatic rigour and conversely greater inclusive capacity. All this had a substantial effect on the concept of nudity.

The fundamental figure in what we might call the transfiguration of nudity, which over time would lead to its negation, was Louis Kahn. And yet Kahn's early work was explicitly naked. In 1943 Kahn wrote an essay entitled "Monumentality" in which he asserted: "The giant major skeleton of the structure can assert its right to be seen. It need no longer be clothed for eye appeal".[60] In support of this peremptory declaration Kahn made drawings in which the monumental centre of a hypothetical city was entrusted to imposing skeletal cantilever canopy that took the Miesian principle of the naked skeleton as manifestation of an intrinsic truth to an even greater extreme. The project for the Richards Medical Towers in Philadelphia (1952–57) translated the ideas put forward in "Monumentality" into an architecture of great effect. The tower, which looks like a megastructure, is a concrete skeleton made up of a grid of pillars set at an angle that have capitals in their intersections housing services and stores. As it rises, the complex vertical structure encounters thin floor slabs of prestressed reinforced concrete. It is revealing that Kahn intended to clad this skeleton with panels, but that they were never installed as they would have nullified the beauty of the naked skeleton. The design was greatly influenced by the contribution of Kahn's collaborator Anne Tyng, who had been working for some time on the idea of a complex structure capable of moulding simultaneously both the image of the building and its space. An idea that ran all the way through the fifties, from Mies onwards, but that with Richard Buckminster Fuller and Konrad Wachsmann took on ever more extreme and complex forms. In this regard Tyng spoke explicitly of a skeletal order on which to apply "corporeal" architectural forms.[61] So in the early days order, which was to obsess Kahn throughout his career, corresponded to structure in an even more clear-cut manner than for Mies, for whom order and even structure always retained something of the intangible. At the end of the fifties, as if he had a vision, Kahn abandoned structural order and felt and made his own the force of the wall and the power of its patterns of light and shade: a definitive choice, which marked a distancing from the Modern Movement that was to change the course of architecture. At the outset his fascination was a romantic one: the wall was seen in fact as a solitary and minimal apparition from which to deduce what amounted to an ancestral mysticism.[62] In its later developments this apparition tended to be structured into increasingly complex articulations, in a true budding of wall structures, always based on the Beaux-Arts principle of axial composition. So the result was a composition of walls that enclose other walls, or rather, as Vincent Scully points out quoting Kahn

himself, one that involved "wrapping buildings with ruins".[63] The Bangladesh Parliament Building in Dacca (1962–73) is an example of this approach on a monumental scale in which a core is covered with a ring of other walls that as a whole configure an envelope which has lost any relationship with its original nucleus. Inevitably, with the affirmation of the principle of the envelope the needs of the image gained the upper hand and the Dacca Parliament, with its laconic and undefined historical reference, became the symbol of a period that, after fifty years of iconoclasm, has increasingly been drawn to evocative, even fairy-tale images.

The Decline of Naked Architecture

Thus Kahn liberalized the principle of the envelope and implicitly with it the license to "dress" a building as one pleased. The transformation of his own architecture over time was radical: setting out from the search for a relationship of intrinsic necessity between structure and space, it turned, through the fascination of ruined walls, into the packaging of evocative images. All this without any particular theoretical strategy, in an almost wholly unconscious manner. The first to become aware of Kahn's "unwitting" revolution was Robert Venturi. In 1966 Venturi, Kahn's assistant and collaborator although only for a brief period, wrote a book that as Vincent Scully rightly predicted in his introduction to the work, would have an importance comparable to that of Le Corbusier's *Vers une architecture*.[64] *Complexity and Contradiction in Architecture*, the book in question, is presented in a similar way to *Vers une architecture*: both are based on the comparative analysis of images, but while in Le Corbusier's text the thesis was that of an efficient, simple and naked spirit of the time, Venturi put forward a diametrically opposite thesis. The preface of the book consists of a "courteous" manifesto in which the author declares that he loves the complexity and contradiction typical of an architecture that is hybrid and impure (especially the Mannerist kind), but at the same time one capable of finding, as T. S. Elliot would have put it, a "difficult" unity in complexity. To tell the truth an improbable unity, that Venturi himself would never succeed in finding.[65] So Venturi's attack, courteous but uncompromising, was directed at the nudity of form and consequent reductionism of the Modern Movement, which had conquered the United States some years before, imposing a chaste style that was little suited to the vitality of post-war Amer-

Robert Venturi,
Denise Scott Brown,
Steven Izenour
Decorated shed,
from *Learning from
Las Vegas*, 1972

ica. *Complexity and Contradiction* is a learned book, in which the author displays a remarkable knowledge of even minor works of architecture of the past, almost as if he wanted to demonstrate that the time of enthusiasm for the degree zero in modern architecture (as called for by Morris, Loos, Le Corbusier and Mies) was over. In addition, although Venturi does not speak of it explicitly, the text rediscovers the principle of decoration, which only a few in modern times (Piranesi and Morris among them) had had the courage to defend.[66]

An essential point, almost a postulate, of the new inclusive architecture invoked by Venturi is the critique of the modernist axiom of the correspondence between interior and exterior of the building, to which Venturi devotes the ninth chapter of the book.[67] In this connection Venturi cites Alvar Aalto's Maison Carré (1955) as an example of how it is possible to remain modern while not respecting the postulates of Modernist orthodoxy. Thus with Venturi the principle of dressed architecture or the envelope, with its ability to present a disjuncted image between inside and outside, acquired theoretical validity.[68] By this time Venturi was openly using the envelope in his projects, as is demonstrated by the house at Chestnut Hill (1957), whose tectonic sense prefigures much of the architecture that was to come and that would find its fulfilment thirty years later in Rem Koolhaas's theory of Bigness.[69] The premises of *Complexity and Contradiction* were taken further in his next book, *Learning from Las Vegas* (1972), written with Denise Scott Brown and Steve Izenour. While *Complexity and Contradiction* owes a great deal to Gestalt theory, much in vogue at the time it was written, *Learning from Las Vegas* is indebted instead to semiotics and the analysis of signs. As is well-known, its thesis is that Las Vegas is a city where the buildings count for little. What matters and what characterizes the city is rather the decorative system of advertising signs that cover the essentially nondescript boxes of the buildings. So the city's character does not stem from its constructions, but from what is affixed to them, an apparently simple system that actually follows extremely sophisticated principles and rules. With more specific regard to the building, the authors develop the theory of the decorated shed, of the façade applied to an anonymous box that distinguishes the building and allows it to become a means of commercial communication and as a consequence part of urban daily experience.[70] So while *Complexity and Contradiction* had legitimized the envelope on the scale of the building, *Learning from Las Vegas* legitimized it, through the concept of the decorated shed, on an urban scale.

The hypothesis of Venturi was endorsed by many of those involved in the international debate, and on the line drawn by Kahn of a direct reappraisal of history a rupture with the Modern soon occurred, inevitably bringing with it the rejection of nudity, now seen as an expression of coercion and inhibition. Several years after Venturi Robert Stern wrote: "[...] buildings have façades which tell stories. These façades are not the diaphanous veil of orthodox Modern architecture, nor are they the affirmation of deep structural secrets. They are mediators between the building as a "real" construct and those illusions and perceptions necessary to put the building in closer touch with the place in which it is made and beliefs and dreams of the architects who designed it, the clients who paid for it, and the civilization which permitted it to be built".[71]

The new sensibility expressed in Stern's words became particularly dominant in the United States, as is shown by the evolution of the debate in one of the most influential magazines of the period, *Perspecta*.[72] The articles published in its many issues, all of authoritative level, reflect a process in which the interest shifted from an initial focus on space to one on structure, arriving through the rather flirtatious modern mannerism of Johnson or Yamasaki at a rediscovery of history and a championing of the new theories of communication, all in a very short space of time. Kahn and then Johnson, Moore, Scully, Venturi, Jenks and Stern manipulated the precepts of Modern orthodoxy to the point of making them unrecognizable, or rather increasingly recognizable as a direct attack on nudity and on its pretensions to represents a moral and ethical superiority. This attack was translated by Peter Blake, and especially by Tom Wolfe, into a biting journalistic language with populist tones: for these authors naked architecture was the expression of a neurosis derived from a cultural subjection that had become in the course of time a cumbersome fashion, the appanage of an élite steeped in politically correct conformism.[73]

In Europe the attack to nudity came primarily from Italy, a country where, except among the Futurists, naked architecture has never proved particularly popular. Paolo Portoghesi was in the front line of this drumhead trial of nudity. His book *After Modern Architecture*[74] sums up the traits of a new tendency that were to find their apotheosis in 1980 with the Venice Biennale of Architecture, curated by Portoghesi himself, in which each architect invited to take part was asked to create a façade for a model street that at the time might have appeared to represent the definitive victory of the decorated shed and envelopes over naked architecture.[75] That nudity had become a negative value in the eighties is evident from the fact that even architects like Richard Meier, Peter Eisenman or John Hejduk, whose aim was to start out again from Le Corbusier's Purism, made use of the envelope in construction, thereby turning the Spartan works of the twenties from essentially naked buildings into ones dressed with a sophistication verging on affectation. There were few exceptions to dressed architecture in those years. Among them were the works of Aldo Rossi, whose terse and anti-decorative architecture, founded on a skeletal composition of an Enlightenment flavour, seems to be based on the principles of nudity. But it is an illusion: Rossi's architecture looks naked, but it is not. In fact Rossi was wholly uninterested in the structural logic of the building and agreed, although in his own way, with the majority of the architects of the time on the fact that inside and outside could be separated. Nudity for him, through the notion of type, was reduced to an icon, to an expression halfway between the Platonic and the sentimental that has very little to do with the objective and moral nudity that had characterized the Modern Movement.[76]

A quote from Oscar Wilde captures the sense of a period that from Kahn onwards increasingly rejected the nudity of buildings. Wilde wrote: "The more one analyses people, the more all reasons for analysis disappear. Soon-

Pier Luigi Nervi
with Annibale Vitellozzi
Palazzetto dello Sport
under construction,
1954–58

er or later one comes to that dreadful universal thing called human nature".[77] If we substitute buildings for the term people it is clear that the architecture of envelopes was a reaction to the modern "good intention" of finding the way back to the Garden of Eden through the myth of the naked and sincere building. From the sixties onwards this myth was viewed in a negative light, and thus Wilde's "dreadful thing" became Laugier's primitive hut, which for the first time appeared, in its overweening pride, naked, indecent, and absolutely in need of clothing. The long season of envelopes, which stretches from Venturi to Koolhaas, and coincides with Postmodernism, is now drawing to an end.[78]

Engineering and Naked Architecture

There is a clear, even obvious relationship between nudity and engineering.[79] It is well-known that, as soon as it appeared at the end of the 18th century, engineering revolutionized architecture; the rational and intuitive "chaste beauty" of iron bridges and constructions had the effect of an apparition to which architecture attempted to respond, but with considerable difficulty. Among the few exceptions to this impasse was the reaction of Viollet-le-Duc, who was able to go beyond facile infatuation or equally facile denigration by proposing, through an analytical analysis of its elements, the first fully technical architectural style. In general, up until the second half of the last century engineering and nudity switched roles, becoming blurred. Evidence of this is provided by one of the key texts of modern historiography, Nikolaus Pevsner's *Pioneers of the Modern Movement* (1943), which devotes a chapter to this troubled relationship; its first image is that of the interior of an 18th-century British factory: a naked spatial volume, studded with a series of elegant iron pillars, nothing else, as if intending to demonstrate the coincidence of the two components.[80] In the images that follow (warehouses, iron bridges, glasshouses, works by the Chicago School, early works of architecture in reinforced concrete) this coincidence is lost and Pevsner, like others after him, has a great deal of difficulty in identifying the links between technical construction and architecture. More complex, but still not convincing, is the interpretation put forward by Sigfried Giedion (1941), which starts from the iron constructions of the 19th century and arrives at what in his view is the key figure, Robert Maillart, to whom he devotes a chapter with the significant title "Construction and Aesthetics: Slab and Plane".[81] His argument is that Maillart's reinforced-concrete bridges, in which the elements are reduced to slab and plane, can be seen as the translation of avant-garde languages, and in particular Neo-Plasticism, in a technical key. The validity of this argument is questionable: in fact technical constructions (and this is still true today) has only marginally, and as it were unconsciously, been influenced by systems of composition, following instead its own by and large anti-compositional road. Yet it is interesting to note that Giedion, like Pevsner before, illustrates the beginning of the chapter with the image of an industrial interior in bare reinforced concrete constructed by Robert Maillart in 1910. For Giedion therefore, as for Pevsner and to a certain extent for Zevi too,[82] nudity and engineering coincided, at least at the beginning of the Modern era.

After the Second World War, in what has fittingly been regarded as the golden age of engineering, this coincidence tended to wane and the technical structure, developing a system of its own forms, emancipated itself from architecture to the point of competing with it. Reyner Banham appropriately subdivides the engineering of that period on the basis of two distinct interpretations: that of the space-structure and that of the plastic structure.[83] To the first group belong Buckminster Fuller and Wachsmann, who worked on light modular structures and on their ability to shape ever larger spaces in new and radical forms. Kahn's aforementioned Richards Medical Towers were certainly influenced by the engineering of the space-structure, a tendency that in the second half of the sixties would spread from the United States and be adopted by radical European groups. The plastic structure provided a different interpretation, which instead of using lightweight materials preferred to work with reinforced concrete, a material that in those very years underwent considerable development as a result of research into the resistance provided by the form of structures (thin vaults) and prestressing. Edoardo Torroja, Pier Luigi Nervi and Félix Candela were the most prominent exponents of a tendency going back to Freyssinet and especially Maillart, and that found expression in a construction made up of slabs, domes and cantilevers whose aim was to make

Steven Holl with Guy
Nordenson
Simmons Hall Building,
1999–2002
Cambridge, MA, USA

the structure coincide as far as possible with the final form, with a view to creating an architecture of pure space enclosed by a naked structure. Their boldness, immediacy, rigour and of course technical fascination meant that plastic structures attained considerable success in those years, influencing with their poetics of *béton brut* or raw reinforced concrete the new course taken by Le Corbusier and the Brutalist movement. But the success was to be short-lived: already in the second half of the sixties the advent of envelopes, combined with the rediscovery of history and regional languages, undermined the very reasons for plastic structures. If the plastic structure went into decline, however the space-structure demonstrated greater staying power. The legacy of Buckminster Fuller and Wachsmann was taken up by Frei Otto, but in this case too, notwithstanding Frei Otto and Günther Behnisch's exploit of the Munich Olympic Stadium (1972), there was a sudden decline in favour. What emerged instead was an alternative to the space-structure and the plastic structure in which it was not so much the structure that was highlighted, as the technical elements of construction.[84] This was the high-tech style, a tendency that even in the years of the Postmodernism, generally hostile to technical expressivity, acquired a certain prominence, especially in the English-speaking world. With high-tech we are now a long way away from naked architecture; if anything it would be more logical to speak of architecture dressed (if not decorated) with technology. In the same years the role of the engineer changed as well: the figure of the engineer-architect, typical of the fifties and sixties, was replaced by that of the engineer of components who, like Peter Rice, worked not so much on the overall form as on the engineering of that form, concentrating on the definition of its individual parts and the engineering of their production.[85] So in the years in which architecture was dressed, engineering contributed by providing it with one of its many garments, made up of a profusion of technical equipment. This continued until the appearance of Santiago Calatrava who, indifferent to high-tech and components in general, went back to working on the overall form, becoming an architect-engineer again. In doing so he carried out a true revolution in that he undermined what had previously been two taboos of structural design: rigorism, which required a relationship of rational interdependence between form and structure, and typicality, i.e. the possibility of reproducing any structure. In fact Calatrava's designs represent an expressive kind of engineering, one that, based on analogy, owes a great deal to Gaudí, to the idea of the structure as a living body, and translates into an effort to come up with a form capable of creating the illusion of movement.[86] The result is a highly distinctive style, almost an oneiric Gothic, made up of sculptural bones and bodies in plastic tension as if they were on the point of springing to life. Calatrava's vision had a similar effect on engineering to the one Venturi had had on architecture: his subjective and metaphorical forms showed that a discipline thought to be wholly constrained by technical considerations and calculation was able to transcend them and manipulate them to obtain particular sculptural effects. Thus with Calatrava engineering discovered that the aim was not so much that "constructing correctly" of which Pier Luigi Nervi had spoken before[87] as communicating with the public and captivating it. While for Venturi this task had been left to the decorated shed, Calatrava saw that it could be done by the emphasized, almost baroque structure.

So there is an engineering before and after Calatrava, and the most significant exponent of the latter is certainly Cecil Balmond. An engineer and fellow of Ove Arup, one of the most renowned engineering and design firms in the world, Balmond has collaborated with a whole series of architects and made a decisive contribution to realizing their ideas. In parallel he has developed a poetic of his own based on the formal independence of the structure, which through an exploration of abstract patterns (from the most elementary to fractals) is able to evoke natural forms.[88] The principle is the same as the one put forward earlier by Frei Otto, that the form is not a priori, but the fruit of a process that in order to be innovative and expressive must necessarily start out from the "informal".[89] In fact this distances engineering yet again from naked architecture, which as we have seen is founded on premises of simplicity and immediacy that have very little to do with the exaltation of formal complexity in Balmond's works. Over the last decade the engineering of the informal, of the form a posteriori obtained through a process in which digital technologies play a decisive role, has enjoyed considerable success, at least from a theoretical point of view. Titles like *Autogenetic Structures* or *The New Structuralism* are indicative of an orientation that has set itself the goal of becoming a new avant-garde, but one that increasingly runs the risk of lapsing into involutional formalism.[90]

The fact remains that the new engineering, after Calatrava, has played an essential role in the transformation of envelopes. Through a series of noteworthy buildings of recent years it is possible to identify the course of what it is appropriate to regard as a genuine metamorphosis that has effectively led to naked architecture. The first significant project in this respect was the Jussieu Library (1992), in which Rem Koolhaas worked with Cecil Balmond on the development of a skeleton whose floor slabs become rampant planes that house the volumes; as Kahn had done for the Towers in Philadelphia, Koolhaas did not show the facing, a sign that the interest had shifted back onto what the latter contains. Another significant moment is Toyo Ito's Sendai Mediathèque (2000–03). In this case the structure, studied by Mutsuro Sasaki, once again determines the image of the building. It is composed of a series of groups of pillars bound together that run the whole height of the building and that look like algae in an aquarium. Here the envelope has become transparent again, revealing an internal structure of great metaphorical value. In the same years as Ito and Sasaki built the media library Guy Nordenson, one of the most respected of contemporary engineers, collaborated with Steven Holl on the construction of the Simmons Hall students' dormitory at MIT (1999–2002), developing a prefabricated cellular load-bearing façade able to absorb the projections and hollows called for by the design. The hypothesis of an expressive structural façade was also explored by Bernard Tschumi in a significant building for Cincinnati University (2003–06). These buildings show how envelopes have over time regained their thickness, and with it an ever greater

Toyo Ito with
Mutsuro Sasaki
Sendai Mediathèque,
1995–2000
Sendai, Japan

structural dignity; in the meantime the cladding materials are being drawn once again from the world of building, so that the "skins" that were all the rage in the early years of the new century are now only to be found in the more vulgar buildings. The innovation of this new season, which we could define as that of structural envelopes, is decoration. As we have seen, engineering from Calatrava onwards has grown increasingly concerned with form, and effectively with image: the works of Balmond and Sasaki and the theoretical formulations of Farshid Moussavi and Michael Kubo express the phenomenon fully.[91] Exemplary in this respect is Herzog and de Meuron's stadium for the Beijing Olympics (2006–08), which consists of a metaphorical drawing translated into structure. Thus the transformation of envelopes has been a prelude to today's naked architecture, although it then distanced itself from the latter with its emphasis on decoration.

The Current Return of Naked Architecture

It would be a mistake to think that naked architecture had completely disappeared during the period when the architecture of envelopes held sway. In Latin America for instance, and Brazil in particular, it is legitimate to speak of a genuine tradition of naked architecture. Its founder was undoubtedly Oscar Niemeyer who even before the war, moving from Le Corbusier's succinct bird's-eye drawings of the city of the thirties, had created a language in which the architecture itself seems to have been reduced to a sketch, as if it were possible to cancel out the distance between the latter and its realization.[92] A hypothesis that Niemeyer has investigated throughout his career, centred on what we might define as an iconographic nudity that in the work of two other Brazilian architects, João Vilanova Artigas and Paulo Mendes de Rocha, is expressed with a denser and more material plasticity than Niemeyer's. These authors, like many other South Americans, deliberately make use of nudity as the expression of a socially engaged and responsible attitude in search of a comprehensible, terse and in some ways popular modern language. The case of the naked tradition in Switzerland is different, more specifically based on the configuration of the architectural object, and in particular its tectonics. There are two sources of this tradition: the legacy of Gottfried Semper and that of Swiss engineers, from Maillart onwards.[93]

Some works can also be considered precursors of today's naked architecture: Enric Miralles and Carme Pinós's Olympic Archery Range in Barcelona (1992) and Rem Koolhaas's House in Bordeaux (1998): works that are quite different but have parallels. In both the structural system tallies with the overall sense of the building, in both the finishings are kept to a minimum and, in contrast to what Venturi had advised, in both the internal and external appearance of the building coincide. Then, if there is a date or rather a work to which the rediscovery of naked architecture can be ascribed, it is the inauguration of the Palais de Tokyo in Paris (2001). Lacaton and Vassal, its designers, did not in fact renovate the historic building, but simply left it as if it were a naked construction site, an unfinished work fitted out with light structures, as if it were an exterior. Since that moment naked architecture has developed piecemeal, without

a precise programme, talking routes that are different but all share the following characteristics:

Anne Lacaton
& Jean-Philippe Vassal
Renovation of the Palais
de Tokyo, 2001
Paris

- the tendency to favour structural parts over facings;
- the tendency to keep finishings to a minimum, making rustic surfaces expressive;
- the desire to find a structural and stylistic analogy between inside and outside;
- the quest for an expressive simplicity that can be perceived with immediacy;
- distrust of architecture as expression of a method of composition;
- a disaffection with intellectual constructions in support of the practice of architecture

In this essay I have brought together a series of works of recent years that in my view fully express these characteristics; an operation that I have carried out in line with Le Corbusier's twofold interpretation of nudity: white (elevated and rich), and grey (humble and frugal). The division into six categories (four white and two grey) with which the works are presented is not an end, but a means of making the very notion of nudity less elusive.

It is clear, as the reader will have realized, that I sympathize with the motives of an architecture that lays itself bare, that tired of itself is seeking a degree zero with which to go back to expressing its justifications if nothing else. I concur with both its formal results and its symbolic implications. But above and beyond personal preferences the fact remains that nudity in architecture is one of the few terms that have the capacity to link the language of architects with that of ordinary people. For this, at least, it should be appreciated. For the rest the words of Giorgio Agamben may ring true: "[...] nudity, that, like a treble voice, signifies nothing and, for this very reason, pierces us".[94]

[1] Where nudity in architecture is concerned it is worth considering the words used by Roland Barthes to describe the Eiffel Tower, not coincidentally one of the prototypes of naked architecture: "[...] it develops much more general symbols, belonging to that order of total sensations, at once powerful and vague, generated not by a particular sense, such as sight or hearing, but by the deep life of the body [...] all the great archetypes of sensation are mixed up here and in the end consecrate the tower as poetic effect". Roland Barthes, *La Tour Eiffel* (Paris: Delpire, 1964). The passage has been translated from the Italian edition, *La Tour Eiffel* (Milan: Abscondita, 2009), pp. 42–3.

[2] Giorgio Agamben, *Nudities*, trans. by David Kishik and Stefan Pedatella (Palo Alto (CA): Stanford University Press, 2010); original edition: *Nudità* (Rome: Nottetempo, 2009).

[3] Octavio Paz, *Appearance Stripped Bare*, trans. by Rachel Phillips and Donald Gardner (New York: Viking Press, 1978); original edition: *Apariencia desnuda* (Mexico City: Era, 1966).

[4] See Sally O'Reilly, *The Body in Contemporary Art* (London: Thames and Hudson, 2009).

[5] On the subject of ruins and their relationship with nudity see Hans Sedlmayr, *Art in Crisis: The Lost Centre* (Piscataway, New Jersey: Transaction Publishers, 2006); original edition: *Verlust der Mitte* (Salzburg: Otto Müller Verlag, 1948). See too Georg Simmel, "The Ruin", in *Georg Simmel, 1858–1919: A Collection of Essays*, ed. and trans. by Kurt Wolff (Columbus: Ohio State University Press, 1959), pp. 259–66.

Franco Purini has also written on the theme: "The ruin is not just a mental and poetic locus dear to architects, for in it is summed up a profound meditation that has as its subjects time, the defeat of human illusions and nature that takes back possession of the land which had been violated by the construction: its enigmatic centrality derives from Vitruvius's definition of architecture as a combination of *utilitas*, *firmitas* and *venustas*, i.e. utility, solidity and beauty. A consequence of this famous definition is that beauty can never be appreciated alone, as it is always accompanied by function and by structural stability. To really contemplate it in an isolation that emphasizes [its beauty] it is necessary for the construction to no longer have a function and for it to be destroyed. This is precisely the condition of the ruin. In it the times of design curve around a superimposition of childhood and old age, in an ideal and mysterious suspension". Franco Purini, *Comporre l'architettura* (Rome-Bari: Laterza, 2000), pp. 59–60.

[6] On this see *Goethe's Way of Science. A Phenomenology of Nature*, eds. by David Seamon and Arthur Zajonc (New York: SUNY Series, Environmental & Architectural Phenomenology, State University of New York Press, 1998). The concept of nudity appears several times in Baudelaire's writings, in particular in "The Painter of Modern Life", in *The Painter of Modern Life and Other Essays*, ed. and trans. by Jonathan Mayne (London: Phaidon, 2006), and *My Heart Laid Bare*, trans. by Ariana Reines (New York: Mal-O-Mar, 2009).

[7] Colin Rowe, *The Architecture of Good Intentions* (London: Academy Editions, 1994), p. 43.

[8] On the mythology of the loss of Paradise for architecture see Joseph Rykwert, *On Adam's House in Paradise* (Cambridge, MA: The MIT Press, 1972). See too Mircea Eliade, *Briser le toit de la maison: La creativité et ses symbols* (Paris: Gallimard, 1986).

[9] On the aspiration to purity in modern architecture as an expression of truth see the chapter "Truth" in Adrian Forty, *Words and Buildings: a Vocabulary of Modern Architecture* (London: Thames & Hudson, 2000), pp. 289–310. Interesting in this connection is Hans Sedlmayr's argument that the purity inherent in modern architecture emerged in the 19th century as part of a more general desire for autonomy on the part of the individual arts, and first of all architecture; Hans Sedlmayr, *op. cit.*, pp. 120–35.

[10] Bruno Zevi, "Il grado zero della scrittura architettonica", in *Pretesti di critica architettonica* (Turin: Einaudi, 1983), pp. 273–9. See too Roland Barthes, *Writing Degree Zero*, trans. by Annette Lavers and Colin Smith (New York: Hill and Wang, 1968); original edition: *Le degré zéro de l'écriture* (Paris: Éditions du Seuil, 1953).

[11] "[...] moreover in the face of an extreme formalization of our existence in an increasingly rationalized world that has its roots in the Enlightenment, there is an equally total materialization of the other, a general biologization or somatization, an understanding by humanity that the meaning of our existence is nothing but our corporeality: body am I entirely, and nothing else as Zarathustra declared". Bernhard Casper, in *Il Sole 24 ore*, cultural supplement of 27 June 2010.

[12] "In the arts there is an essential beauty [...] we feel this beauty to be essential, but we have difficulty in defining it; it is an allure that attracts us, the feeling of pleasure persists,

while the idea of the thing escapes us; the heart is sure of itself, but the mind is not always able to explain it [...]. [Beauty] is often abandoned out of prejudice or fashion, while we always return to it through sensation and reason". Marc-Antoine Laugier, *Essai sur l'Architecture* (Paris: 1751). The passage has been translated from the Italian ed., *Saggio sull'architettura*, ed. by Vittorio Ugo (Palermo: Aesthetica Edizioni, 1987), p. 162.

[13] On the evolution of the idea of the primitive hut as developement of an idea see the chapters "Truth" and "Structure" in Adrian Forty, *op. cit.*, pp. 276–87 and pp. 289–302.

[14] Francesco Milizia, *Memorie degli Architetti Antichi e Moderni* (Parma: Stamperia Reale, 1781). The passage is cited by Joseph Rykwert in *On Adam's House in Paradise, op. cit.*

[15] These concepts crop up several times, especially in relation to the crisis in traditional composition, in Kaufmann's book on Enlightenment and revolutionary architects: Emil Kaufmann, *Architecture in the Age of Reason* (Cambridge, MA: Harvard University Press, 1955).

[16] William J. R. Curtis, *Modern Architecture since 1900* (London: Phaidon Press, 1987), p. 24. Moreover in 1828 Hübsch also declared that "we must not overlay bare yet functional walls with feigned constructions"; cited in Hans Sedlmayr, *op. cit.*

[17] Leopold Eidlitz, *The Nature and Function of Art* (1881), cited in Adrian Forty, *op. cit.*, p. 258.

[18] "The ideas of appearance and separation between structural elements and filling elements; the idea of free composition stemming from a process of simple addition; the idea of dynamic, tense and active elements contrasted with other passive, static and complementary ones: these are all ideas in which the Gothic model and the technology born out of the industrial revolution have points of contact". Ignasi de Solà-Morales, "Viollet-le-Duc e l'architettura moderna", in *Archeologia del Moderno: da Durand a Le Corbusier* (Turin: Allemandi, 2005), p. 89. On the figure of Viollet-le-Duc in general see Kenneth Frampton, "Greco-Gothic and Neo-Gothic: The Anglo-French Origins of Tectonic Form", in *Studies in Tectonic Culture: The Poetics of Construction in Nineteenth and Twentieth Century* (Cambridge, MA: The MIT Press, 1999).

[19] See Harry Mallgrave, *Gottfried Semper: Architect of the Nineteenth Century* (New Haven: Yale University Press, 1996).

[20] Gottfried Semper, *The Four Elements of Architecture and Other Writings*, trans. by Harry Mallgrave and Wolfgang Herrmann (New York: Cambridge University Press, 1989).

[21] Taking up Semper's ideas in his *Die Tektonik* (1874), Karl Bötticher divided the construction into *Kernform*, core or intrinsic form, and *Kunstform*, artistic and symbolic form.

[22] Kenneth Frampton, *op. cit.*

[23] "Konrad Fiedler, in an 1878 essay that took its starting point in Semper's theory, suggested a peeling away of the dressing of antique architecture to express in modern works the wall's full spatial possibility. This suggestion was taken up and developed by August Schmarsow in a 1893 lecture, in which he specifically rejected the decorative attributes of the "art of dressing" (*Bekleidungskunst*) in favor of architecture's abstract capacity to create space" (*Raumgestaltung*). The history of architecture is now to be analyzed as a 'feeling for space' (*Raumgefühl*)." Harry Mallgrave, introduction to *The Four Elements of Architecture and Other Writings*, cited in Kenneth Frampton, *op. cit.*

[24] On the debate over these themes at the time see: Ignasi de Solà-Morales, "Per un museo moderno: da Riegl a Giedion", in Id., *op. cit.*, pp. 177–91. See too: Harry Mallgrave (with Eleftherios Ikonomou), *Empathy, Form, and Space: Problems in German Aesthetics 1873–1893* (Santa Monica: Getty Publication Programs, 1994).

[25] The term proto-rationalist was used by Edoardo Persico and explicitly taken up by Renato De Fusco in *Storia dell'architettura contemporanea* (Rome-Bari: Laterza, 2007), p. 63 (1st ed. Laterza, 1974).

[26] Sigfried Giedion, *Space, Time and Architecture* (Cambridge, MA: Harvard University Press, 1941), p. 292.

[27] Hendrik Petrus Berlage, *Gedanken über Stil in der Baukunst* (Leipzig: 1905). The passage has been translated from the citation in Italian in Giovanni Fanelli and Roberto Gargiani, *Storia della architettura contemporanea* (Rome-Bari: Laterza, 1998), p. 138.

[28] Hendrick Petrus Berlage, "Over de waarschijnlijke ontwikkeling", in *Architectura*, XIII, 1905. Translated from the citation in Giovanni Fanelli and Roberto Gargiani, *op. cit.*, p. 133.

[29] Otto Wagner, *Moderne Architektur*, cited in Sigfried Giedion, *op. cit.*, p. 309.

[30] Giovanni Fanelli, Roberto Gargiani, *op. cit.*, pp. 55–100.

[31] "Otto Wagner, Josef Hoffmann, Joseph Maria

Olbrich and Adolf Loos entrusted the formal definition of architecture to the design of the wall, understood as a graphic surface filled with symbolic and autonomous potential with respect to the structural system". Giovanni Fanelli and Roberto Gargiani, *op. cit.*, p. 55.

[32] Adolf Loos, "The Principle of Cladding", in *Spoken into the Void: Collected Essays 1897–1900*, trans. by Jane O. Newman and John H. Smith (Cambridge, MA-London: The MIT Press, 1982). See too: Juan José Lahuerta, "Adolf Loos: ornamento e delitto?", in *Casabella*, nos. 788 and 789, 2009, and David Leatherbarrow and Mohsen Mostafavi, *Surface Architecture* (Cambridge, MA-London: The MIT Press, 2002).

[33] Renato de Fusco, *op. cit.*, p. 121.

[34] Giovanni Fanelli and Roberto Gargiani, *op. cit.*, p. 127.

[35] Tony Garnier, *Une cité industrielle: étude pour la construction des villes* (New York: Princeton Architectural Press, 1989).

[36] "[I] proclaim [...] that decoration as an element superimposed on architecture is absurd, and that the decorative value of Futurist architecture depends solely on the use and original arrangement of raw or bare or violently coloured materials". Antonio Sant'Elia, *Manifesto of Futurist Architecture*, 1916.

[37] Reyner Banham, *Theory and Design in the First Machine Age* (1960) (Cambridge, MA: The MIT Press, 1980), p. 82. On anonymous industrial architecture and the fascination it exercised on the architects of the Modern Movement see also another of Banham's works: *A Concrete Atlantis: U.S. Industrial Building and European Modern Architecture 1900–1925* (Cambridge, MA: The MIT Press, 1986).

[38] Colin Rowe, "Mannerism and Modern Architecture", in *Mathematics of the Ideal Villa* (Cambridge, MA-London: The MIT Press, 1976), pp. 26–53 (originally published in *Architectural Review*, no. 5, May 1950).

[39] Charles Jenks, *Le Corbusier and the Continual Revolution in Architecture* (New York: The Monacelli Press, 2001).

[40] Cited in Jan de Heer, *The Architectonic Colour: Polychromy in the Purist Architecture of Le Corbusier* (Rotterdam: 010 Publishers, 2009), p. 84; originally published in Willi Boesinger, *Le Corbusier, 1910–1965* (Zurich: Artemis, 1967).

[41] Le Corbusier, *Vers une architecture* (Paris: Édition Crés, 1923).

[42] Henry-Russell Hitchcock and Philip Johnson, *The International Style* (1932) (London-New York: W.W. Norton & Company, 1994), pp. 33–81.

[43] *Le Corbusier & Pierre Jeanneret, œuvre complète 1934-1938*, ed. by Max Bill (Boston-Berlin: Birkhäuser, 1967), p. 131; see too Kenneth Frampton, *op. cit.*

[44] Joseph Rykwert, *op. cit.*, pp. 25–8.

[45] On this see Michelangelo Sabatino, *Pride in Modesty; Modernist Architecture and the Vernacular Tradition in Italy* (Toronto: University of Toronto Press, 2010); G. Pagano, G. Daniel, "Architettura rurale italiana", *Quaderni della Triennale* (Milan: Hoepli, 1936). See Pagano's articles in *Casabella*: "Case rurali", no. 85, February 1935; "Documenti di architettura rurale", no. 95, November 1945; "Architettura rurale in Italia", no. 96, December 1935. On Pagano's photographic reportages see *Giuseppe Pagano fotografo*, ed. by Cesare de Seta (Milan: Electa, 1979).

[46] Francesco Tentori, *Vita e opera di Le Corbusier* (Rome-Bari: Laterza, 1999) pp. 123–35.

[47] Alison and Peter Smithson and Theo Crosby, "The New Brutalism", in *Architectural Design*, vol. 25, January 1955; see too Reyner Banham, *New Brutalism: Ethic or Aesthetic* (London: Reinhold Publishing Corporation, 1966).

[48] Mies van der Rohe, from an article published in *Frülicht*, I, 4, 1922. Cited in *The Presence of Mies*, ed. by Detlef Martins (New York: Princeton Architectural Press, 1994), p. 51. In this respect it is also worth recalling the significant comments made about nudity by Erich Mendelsohn and Walter Gropius, which echo Mies: "The bare bones of the construction force the truth upon us. Where it can still be seen without cladding, the skeleton shows, more clearly and splendidly than the finished building, the boldness of construction with iron or reinforced concrete", Erich Mendelsohn, *Amerika. Bilderbuch eines Architekten* (1926), English ed. *Erich Mendelsohn's "Amerika". 82 Photographs* (Mineola, NY: Dover Publications, 1993), p. 75; "A sound organism requires, just like the human body, a sound bone structure, and what the bone structure represents for the human body is also true for the technical and tectonic part of a building with respect to its overall configuration", Walter Gropius in Fritz Neumeyer, *Mies van der Rohe; le architetture, gli scritti*, ed. by Michele Caja and Mara De Benedetti (Milan: Skira, 2005).

[49] Arthur Drexler, *Ludwig Mies van der Rohe* (New York: George Braziller Inc., 1960).

[50] Michele Caja and Mara De Benedetti, "Nota dei curatori", in Fritz Neumeyer, *op. cit.*, p. 18.

[51] "[What] counts is the essential [...] architecture is not the solution of specific formal problems, even though these may be contained in it", Mies van der Rohe, Lecture given in 1926, in Fritz Neumeyer, *op. cit.*, p. 266.

[52] See Arthur Drexler, *op. cit.*, pp. 22–30. See too Colin Rowe, "Neo-'Classicism' and Modern Architecture II", in Id., *op. cit.*

[53] "Mies developed ideal constructions in the sense of aesthetic metaphors that, with precise eloquence, raised technique to the level of art". William H. Jordy, in his essay "The Laconic Splendor of the Metal Frame", has given a pregnant formulation of Mies's intent. For Jordy the value of Mies's architecture, as required by Nietzsche's aesthetic theory, lay precisely in the way it paraphrased a familiar, almost ordinary theme in search of what Nietzsche called the "everyday melody". William H. Jordy, *American Buildings and Their Architects: The Impact of European Modernism in the Mid-Twentieth Century* (New York: Doubleday 1972), pp. 21–2.

[54] Antonio Monestiroli, "Le forme ed il tempo", in the Italian ed. of Ludwig Hilberseimer's *Mies van der Rohe* (Milan: Città Studi Edizioni, 2001), pp. 13–5.

[55] "The quest for the essential, the simplification of volumes down to the elementary form of the parallelepiped, the spatial unity of the interior, the geometric rigour of the plan, the clarity of the surfaces, the characterization of the walls and structural and functional coherence are the greatest merits that were apparent right from his earliest works of sacred architecture". Giuseppe Zander, *Rudolf Schwarz* (Rome: Edizioni Ente Premi, 1964), p. 20.

[56] Wolfgang Pehnt and Hilde Strohl, *Rudolf Schwarz* (1995), Art Books Intl, Portchester 2000. The passage has been translated from the Italian ed., *Rudolf Schwarz; 1897–1961* (Milan: Electa, 2000), p. 85.

[57] Wolfgang Pehnt and Hilde Strohl, *op. cit.*, p. 97.

[58] Wolfgang Pehnt and Hilde Strohl, *op. cit.*, p. 259.

[59] On the concept of the "great form" see: Fritz Neumeyer, *The Artless Word: Mies van der Rohe on Building Art* (Cambridge, MA: The MIT Press, 1991).

[60] Louis Kahn, "Monumentality", in *Nine Points on Monumentality*, ed. by Sigfried Giedion, Joseph Lluis Sert and Fernand Léger, 1843; now in Sigfried Giedion, *Architecture, You and Me: The Diary of a Development* (Cambridge, MA: Harvard University Press, 1958).

[61] Cited in *Architettura è; Louis Kahn, gli scritti*, ed. by Maria Bonaiti (Milan: Electa, 2002), p. 17.

[62] David B. Brownlee and David G. De Long, *Louis I. Kahn: In the Realm of Architecture* (New York: Rizzoli International, 1991).

[63] Vincent Scully, "Louis I. Kahn and the Ruins of Rome", in Id., *Modern Architecture and Other Essays*, ed. by Neil Levine (Princeton, NJ: Princeton University Press, 2003), p. 311.

[64] Vincent Scully, "Introduction", in Robert Venturi, *Complexity and Contradiction in Architecture* (1966) (New York: The Museum of Modern Art, 1977), pp. 9–11.

[65] Rafael Moneo, *Theoretical Anxiety and Design Strategies in the Work of Eight Contemporary Architects* (Cambridge, MA: The MIT Press, 2004).

[66] On the principle of decoration and its development between the 19th century and the early part of the 20th see for the completeness of its account Nikolaus Pevsner, *Pioneers of Modern Design* (Harmondsworth: Penguin Books, 1991), originally published in 1936 under the title *Pioneers of the Modern Movement*.

[67] "Contrasts between the inside and the outside can be a major manifestation of contradiction in design [...]. Architecture occurs at the meeting of interior and exterior forces of use and space. [...] Architecture as the wall between the inside and the outside becomes the spatial record of this resolution and its drama. And by recognizing the difference between the inside and the outside, architecture opens the door once again to an urbanistic point of view." Robert Venturi, *op. cit.*, pp. 70, 86.

[68] "I tend to design from the outside to the inside, as well as from the inside to the outside; the inevitable tensions contribute to the construction of the architecture. Given that the inside is different from the outside, the point of transition constitutes an architectural event". Jan C. Rowan, "Wanting To Be. The Philadelphia School", in *Progressive Architecture*, April 1961, p. 154.

[69] "In Bigness, the distance between core and envelope increases to the point where the facade can no longer reveal what happens inside. The humanist expectation of 'honesty' is doomed: interior and exterior architectures become separate projects, one dealing with the instability of programmatic and iconographic needs, the other – agent of disinformation – offering the city the apparent stability of an object." Rem Koolhaas, "Bigness or the Problem of Large", in *Small, Medium, Large, Ex-*

tra-Large (New York: The Monacelli Press, 1995).

[70] Robert Venturi, Denise Scott Brown and Steven Izenour, *Learning from Las Vegas* (Cambridge, MA: The MIT Press, 1972).

[71] Robert Stern, *New Directions in American Architecture* (New York: George Braziller Inc., 1969).

[72] In this connection see *Re-Reading Perspecta: The First Fifty Years of the Yale Architectural Journal*, ed. by Robert Stern, Peggy Deamer and Alan Plattus (Cambridge, MA: The MIT Press, 2005).

[73] Peter Blake listed eleven "myths" of the Modern Movement that had caused serious damage to American cities; the third of these myths was that of purity, a myth he challenged from a pragmatic viewpoint, by disputing the poor quality of modern construction materials. Peter Blake, *Form Follows Fiasco: Why Modern Architecture Hasn't Worked* (New York: Atlantic Little, Brown & Co., 1974). See too Tom Wolfe, *From Bauhaus to Our House* (New York: Farrar, Straus & Giroux, 1981).

[74] Paolo Portoghesi, *After Modern Architecture* (New York: Rizzoli, 1982); original edition: *Dopo l'architettura moderna* (Rome-Bari: Laterza, 1980).

[75] See Paolo Portoghesi, "The End of Prohibitionism", and Vincent Scully, "How Things Got to Be the Way They Are Now", in *The Presence of the Past: 1st International Exhibition of Architecture*, Catalogue of the 1980 Biennale (Venice: Edizioni La Biennale, 1981), pp. 9–37.

[76] Rafael Moneo, *op. cit.*

[77] Oscar Wilde, *The Decay of Lying* (1891) (Whitefish, MT: Kessinger Publishing, 2004), p. 7.

[78] On the theme of the Postmodernism as a reinterpretation of the Modern myth of sincerity from Kahn to Baudrillard see "Truth", in Adrian Forty, *op. cit.*, pp. 300–10.

[79] On the specific subject of the relationship between architecture and engineering over time see Andrew Saint, *Architect and Engineer: a Study in Sibling Rivalry* (New Haven-London: Yale University Press, 2007). See too Ivan Margolius, *Architects + Engineers = Structures* (London: Wiley Academy, 2002).

[80] Nikolaus Pevsner, *op. cit.*, p. 141.

[81] Sigfried Giedion, *op. cit.*, p. 450.

[82] Bruno Zevi, *Architettura in nuce* (Venice-Rome: Istituto per la Collaborazione Culturale, 1960), pp. 38–76.

[83] Reyner Banham, *Theory and Design in the First Machine Age, op. cit.*, pp. 79–87.

[84] On the role of technology as language see Reyner Banham, *The Architecture of the Well-Tempered Environment* (London: Architectural Press, 1969).

[85] See Peter Rice, *An Engineer Imagines* (London-Zurich-Munich: Artemis, 1994).

[86] Among the many writings on Calatrava, see: Alexander Tzonis, *Santiago Calatrava, The Poetics of Movement* (New York: Universe Publishing, Rizzoli, 1999); Luca Molinari, *Santiago Calatrava* (Milan: Skira, 1999); Sergio Polano, *Santiago Calatrava* (Milan: Electa, 1997).

[87] Pier Luigi Nervi, *Costruire correttamente* (Milan: Hoepli, 1964).

[88] See Cecil Balmond, *Element* (London: Prestel, 2007). See too *Cecil Balmond*, special issue of *A+U*, November 2006.

[89] Cecil Balmond, "New Structure and the Informal", in *Lotus International*, no. 98, 1998, pp. 70–83; see too Cecil Balmond, *Informal: The Informal in Architecture and Engineering* (London: Prestel, 2002).

[90] Evan Douglis, *Autogenic Structures* (New Yor: Taylor & Francis, 2009). See too "The New Structuralism: Design, Engineering and Architectural Technologies", in *Architectural Design*, no. 206, guest editors: Rivka Oxman and Robert Oxman, July/August 2010.

[91] Farshid Moussavi and Michael Kubo, *The Function of Ornament* (Cambridge, MA-Barcelona: Harvard University Graduate School of Design-Actar, 2006). For the work of Mutsuro Sasaki see Mutsuro Sasaki, *Flux Structure* (Tokyo: Toto, 2005).

[92] Carlos Eduardo Comas, "Niemeyer, el derecho a la diferencia", in *Oscar Niemeyer*, AV Monografías no. 125, 2007. See too Guido Laganà, "Oscar Niemeyer, cento anni", in *Niemeyer 100*, ed. by Guido Laganà and Marcus Lontra (Milan: Electa, 2008), pp. 15–32.

[93] See Gianluca Gelmini, *Architettura Contemporanea, Svizzera* (Milan: Motta/Sole 24 Ore, 2009). On the current state of Swiss engineering see the work of Jürg Conzett: Jürg Conzett and Mohsen Mostafavi, *Structure as Space: Engineering and Architecture in the Works of Jürg Conzett* (London: Architectural Association, 2006); or *Landscape and Structures: a Personal Inventory of Jürg Conzett, Photographed by Martin Linsi* (Zurich: Verlag Scheidegger & Speiss, 2011).

[94] Giorgio Agamben, *op. cit.*, p. 128 (italian edition).

Skeletal Naked Architecture. a bone-like architecture the appearance of which tends to correspond to its structure. Architecture that denudes itself of its cladding or reduces it to a minimum, to the point of revealing a skeleton which with its presence connotes the image of the building. A budding notion of the Modern may be discerned in Leon Battista Alberti. Who was one of the first to suppose an analogy between animal skeletons and buildings, a concept repeated by Perronet and which became a prophecy in 1828 with Heinrich Hübsch, who declared: "A completely objective skeleton for a new style". The prophecy came true with Viollet-le-Duc who drew from Gothic art and translated into Modern the idea of a construction of bones that could resist the forces pressing against it. Architects such as Berlage, Perret, Gropius, Mendelsohn and Le Corbusier were all charmed by the idea of the naked skeleton. Le Corbusier's Maison Domino was the translation into reinforced concrete of Laugier's primitive hut. In the twenties, Mies van der Rohe stated: "Only skyscrapers under construction reveal bold construction ideas and the effect of these steel skeletons that stand out against the sky is overwhelming". After the war, Louis Kahn developed the idea of skeleton to extreme consequences: the Philadelphia tower is nothing other than a skeletal megastructure loaded with volumes; later, opting for walls and the ruins' memory, Kahn abandoned this hypothesis, which would subsequently be borrowed by Archigram in a pop key. But in those same years, Robert Venturi, with his theory of the decorated shed, delegitimized nakedness, which appeared reduced to an icon in the architecture of Aldo Rossi. Today, we are witnessing a revival of skeletal architecture. The new skeletons, however, are different to those of the past; indeed, they have abandoned the claim to representing a structural truth seen as ethical aspiration. What does remain unchanged, if not indeed increased, is the iconographic appeal of the skeleton and its allusion – via the romantic myth of the ruin and of the building under construction – to an unavoidable metaphysics of architecture.

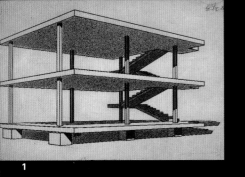

1

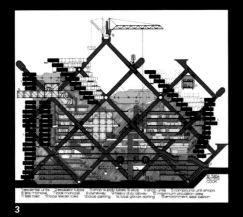

2

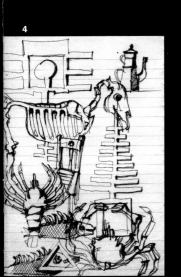

1 residential units   2 escalator tubes   3 shop supply tubes & silos   4 shop units   5 compound unit shops
6 fast monorail   7 local monorail   8 cableway   9 heavy duty railway   10 maximum circulation area
11 fast road   12 local feeder road   13 local parking   14 local goods sorting   15 environment seal balcon

3

4

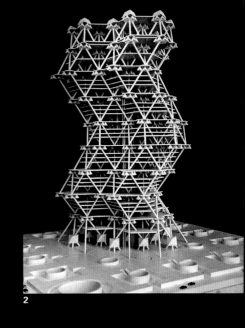

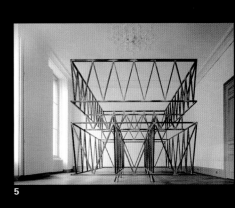

5

National Choreographic Centre

1999–2000
Aix en Provence, France

This work by Rudy Ricciotti from the late nineties can be seen as the forebear of the current trend towards skeletal nakedness in architecture. It dates from the period of greatest success of building envelopes, and despite this has acquired a merited fame. The building (35 x 18 metres) occupies the lot almost entirely and has four floors: the basement houses an auditorium, the foyer and offices are on the first floor, while the two upper floors are left completely free for rehearsal rooms. The vertical load-bearing structure runs up the façade in order to leave the internal space free and takes the form of prefabricated reinforced concrete columns. The general image, midway between unfinished rural buildings and abandoned ones, is appealing and was used several times in the following decade.

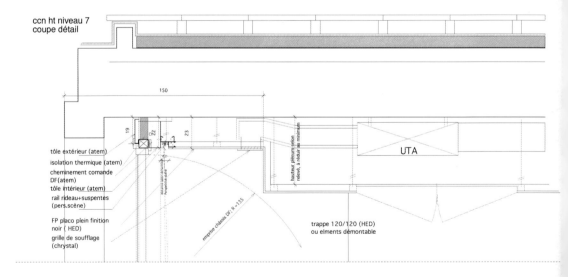

ccn ht niveau 7
coupe détail

150

tôle extérieur (atem)
isolation thermique (atem)
cheminement comande
DF(atem)
tôle intérieur (atem)
rail rideau+suspentes
(pers.scène)

FP placo plein finition
noir (HED)
grille de soufflage
(chrystal)

UTA

trappe 120/120 (HED)
ou elments démontable

North Rhine Westphalia State Offices

2002–03
Berlin, Germany

The building is interesting in that it may be considered a hybrid between building envelope and naked architecture. The concept underlying the work is that of a double structure and double façade; a concept that is not just aesthetic but also has a justification in heat insulation. The interior of the building is essential, at the limit of anonymity, with floors above each other supported by a steel structure. This internal block is enveloped within a case that is structurally and figuratively independent of the rest, a skeletal envelope supported by slender, elegant wooden supports which describe a filigree pattern aiming to communicate the democratic spirit of the new unified Germany through an architectural metaphor.

Steven Holl Architects   **Busan Cinema Complex**

2005
Busan, Korea

This project by Steven Holl recalls Le Corbusier's Tower of Shadows at
Chandigarh with its 75-metre-high skeleton constituting a landmark for the
surrounding area. The large skeleton houses six large rooms that seem laid over
each other in a succession of horizontal slabs. From a structural point of view,
these rooms brace the large naked framework. The same Korean technology as
used to build cargo ships was used for the building: the entire structure is formed
of a sandwich of steel Cor-Ten panels subsequently filled with concrete. Within
these panels run a network of plastic tubes linked to a geothermal system to
assure a balanced thermal comfort throughout the building in summer and winter.

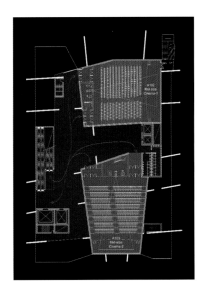

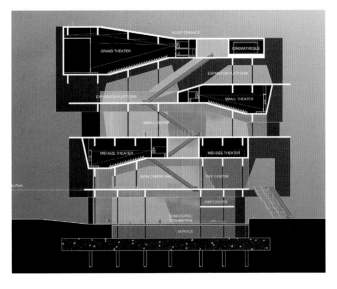

Christian Kerez   **School Building at Leutschenbach**

2002–09
Zurich, Switzerland

This is one of the most expressive examples of current Naked Architecture.
The school appears as an elementary overlay of reinforced concrete floors
supported by a V-shaped steel structure which intensifies on the last floor
and becomes continuous at the top of the building. The last floor, which from
a distance looks like an urban scale lantern, houses the school gym. Although
complex in its static configuration, this building betrays a Spartan character,
reducing the materials used to just three: cement, steel and glass. In this
architecture, the reductionist character of Naked Architecture, arising from
the propensity to stressing the structure to the point of rendering it the image
itself of the building, the almost total elimination of the envelope, the stylistic
similarity between the interior and exterior of the building, is here expressed
with paradigmatic clarity.

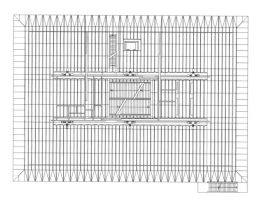
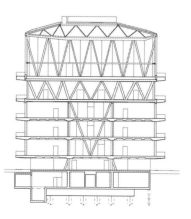

Michel Carlana
Luca Mezzalira
Curzio Pentimalli
Riccardo Sanquerin

Magic Carpet

2010
Montreux, Switzerland

The project expresses an absolute elementariness: a large building with courtyard is placed jutting out from a slope, and to achieve this thrust the entire structure is assimilated into a truss housing the residential area. The architects state: "The idea of a continuous structural element arises from the desire to succeed in outlining a space with a single element: the structure. Nothing is superfluous in the building; the façade is delineated by the structure, giving identity to the final image of the project and making it a symbolic urban element". Particularly interesting is the character of frugal nakedness this rural phalanstery inspires, evidenced by the renderings in which are quoted paintings by Vermeer and Millet.

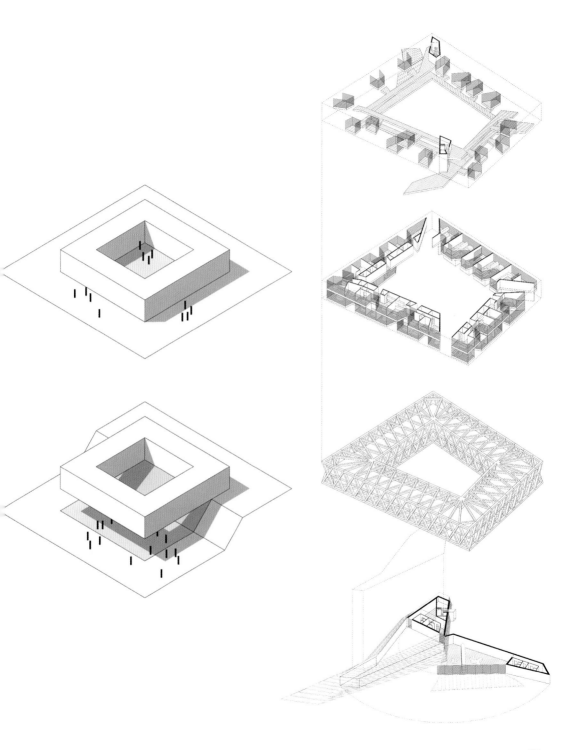

Vakko Fashion Center and Power Media Center

2010
Istanbul, Turkey

An abandoned shell of an unfinished hotel in Istanbul has been completely re-planned by Rex Architects which was required to fulfil the design very quickly. The decision was therefore made to re-use the material for a project in the United States and which had reached the executive stage but was never built, and adapt it to the occasion. In order to speed things up, Rex also chose to divide the intervention into two distinct parts: the first was the existing U-shaped shell, called *Ring*, on which construction began immediately. The second part was the central tower built in the internal courtyard, called *Showcase*: this last was designed while the site for *Ring* was in full swing. It is worth noting the cladding windows rendered rigid by the manipulation of their form, which describes an X alluding to the steel beams of the central tower.

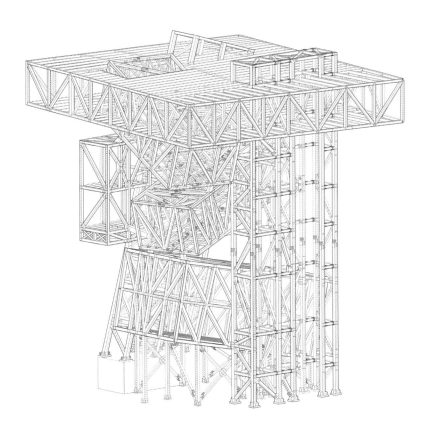

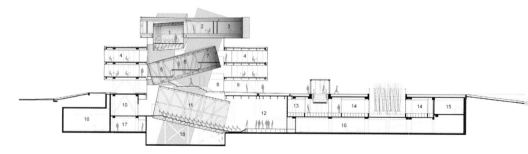

LONGITUDINAL SECTION

1   MEETING ROOM
2   RECEPTION
3   EXECUTIVE OFFICES
4   OFFICES
5   VAKKO BAGS SHOWROOM
6   VAKKO SHIRTS / TIES SHOWROOM
7   VAKKO SCARVES SHOWROOM
8   LOBBY / MUSEUM
9   ENTRANCE

10 AHU ROOM
11 AUDITORIUM
12 TV STUDIO
13 TV PRODUCTION
14 POWER ADMINISTRATIVE OFFICES
15 PARKING RAMP
16 PARKING
17 STORAGE
18 TECHNICAL SERVICE ROOM

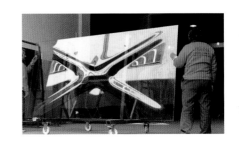

House of Environment of Izadia Ecological Park

2002–07
Anglet, France

The ecological park of Izadia d'Anglet is located at the mouth of the Adour in an area of ponds representing an ecosystem that is unique in France. The House houses the park services and takes the form of a linear structure on stilts, making use of galvanised steel and douglas fir in a large reticular full-height beam running the full length of the building. Within this continuous beam, pavilions alternate with services and panoramic terraces. What is interesting in this work is its character, able to combine two types of nakedness: a rough, rustic one, typical of architecture of an ecological nature, and the linear, serial one of architecture for infrastructure.

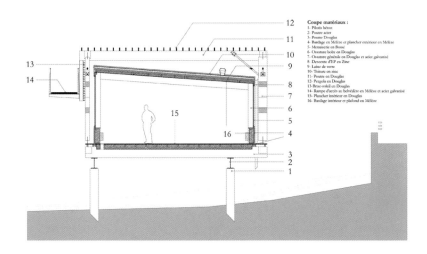

Coupe matériaux :
1- Pilotis béton
2- Poutre acier
3- Poutre Douglas
4- Bardage en Mélèze et plancher extérieur en Mélèze
5- Menuiserie en Bossé
6- Ossature boîte en Douglas
7- Ossature générale en Douglas et acier galvanisé
8- Descente d'EP en Zinc
9- Laine de verre
10- Toiture en zinc
11- Poutre en Douglas
12- Pergola en Douglas
13-Brise-soleil en Douglas
14- Rampe d'accès au belvédère en Mélèze et acier galvanisé
15- Plancher intérieur en Douglas
16- Bardage intérieur et plafond en Mélèze

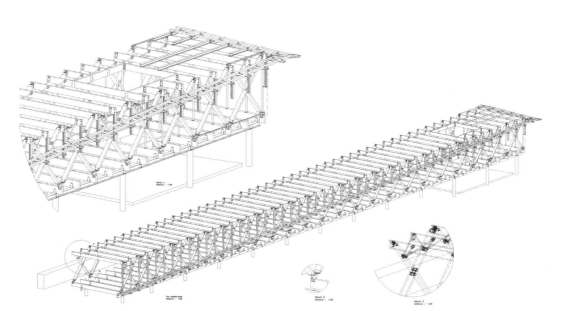

Cecil Balmond   **Weave Bridge**

2008–10
Philadelphia, USA

The outline of the bridge springs from four invisible force-lines that go from
the area of the sports fields and then meet before crisscrossing as they bridge
the gap of 42 metres; it is through the structure that these otherwise invisible
lines materialise. Apart from its iconographic appeal, the elegant bridge maintains
a conventional image similar to the well-known Warren beams, with a single
exception: Balmond's structure has no longitudinal beams. The design has been
determined by the zigzag weave of two spirals that start from the shoulders
of the bridge, and which become thicker in the centre line of the structure.
In this case, the figure of the skeleton acquires a rhythmic quality that avoids
a monotonous mechanical repetition of usual reticular steel beams.

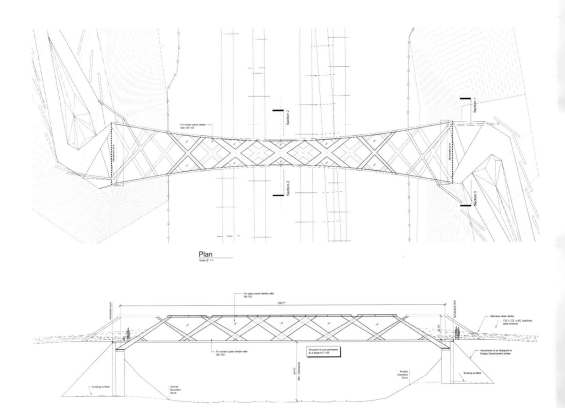

Plan
Scale ⅜" = 1'

Elevation
Scale ⅜" = 1'

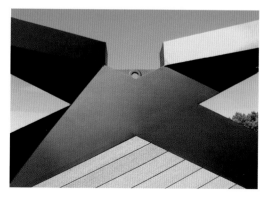

Alberto Mozó

Offices BIP Computers

2006–07
Santiago, Chile

The building is located in a longitudinal lot and is jammed between two small buildings of the thirties. It comprises three floors above ground and a basement floor, all linked by a spiral staircase of great sculptural presence. The construction technique and material correspond to the image of the building: 6 X-shaped columns in untreated timber are set back from the surface of the façade formed of structural walls erected in situ, themselves of untreated timber, and which echo the criss-cross pattern of the interior columns. The floors are also of wood and present a rhythmic, repeated and dense layout of beams and smaller crossbeams. In its elementary clarity, the work offers an excellent example of what we might define a material, rustic skeletal nakedness, which nevertheless has the merit of maintaining a distance from the vernacular.

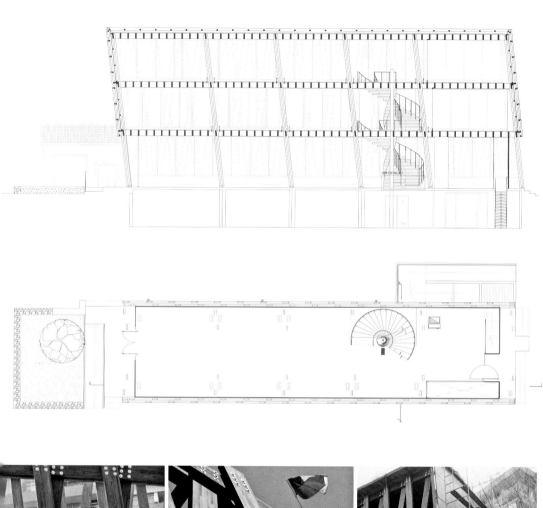

Rough Naked Architecture: naked reinforced concrete architecture, rough, brutalist, radically opposite to a multilayered envelope. In a conference of 1905, Berlage declared that the best material for a "modern" construction is reinforced concrete cast on site as this definitively resolved the conflict between structure and cladding. A few years later, in 1909, the Unity Temple by Frank Lloyd Wright demonstrated the validity of Berlage's hypothesis, and this just a few years before a Futurist, Sant'Elia, affirmed: "The decorative value of Futurist architecture depends only from the use and original disposition of rough or naked (or violently coloured) materials". However, one can only speak of rough nakedness in the fifties when Le Corbusier perfected a plastic expressiveness centred wholly on cast concrete. From the Swiss Pavilion in Paris (1930) to Chandigarh (1950–63), Le Corbusier traced out a development that gave rise to that brutalism anticipated in 1943 by Arancio Williams with an extraordinary bridge house. In *The New Brutalism: Ethic or Aesthetic,* Reyner Banham wrote that brutalism is based on a clear legibility of the layout, an equally visible structure and a use of materials for their raw qualities. A fundamental role in the definition of brutalism in those years was played by the architecture of engineers (Pier Luigi Nervi, Eduardo Torroja and Félix Candela), who used bare reinforced concrete to create fully rounded forms like ribbed domes, shells and hyperboloids, able to resist loads thanks to their form. Today, after years of decline in construction with bare reinforced concrete, we are seeing its revival, and this especially in

1

2

3

4

5

Antón García-Abril

Hemeroscopium House

2005–08
Las Rozas – Madrid,
Spain

A large bare structure formed of an overlay of a series of prefabricated elements which develops upwards in a sequence of elements that become lighter as the structure grows. The order in which these structures are piled up generates a helix that sets out from a stable support, the mother beam. The result is a macroscopic equilibrium of prefabricated elements placed on top of each other, a sort of new version of what Louis Kahn called Viaduct Architecture. The architect says that the calculation and engineering of this structure took a year, while building required only seven days. The meaning of the large prefabricated structure was made clear by the architect himself: "The goal was the invention of a new, effective language in which form disappears, leaving the stage to bare space".

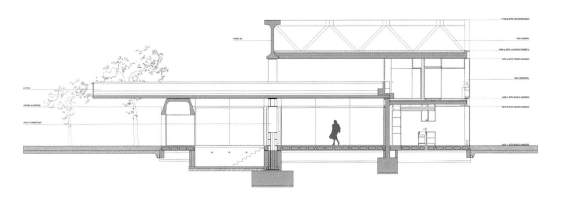

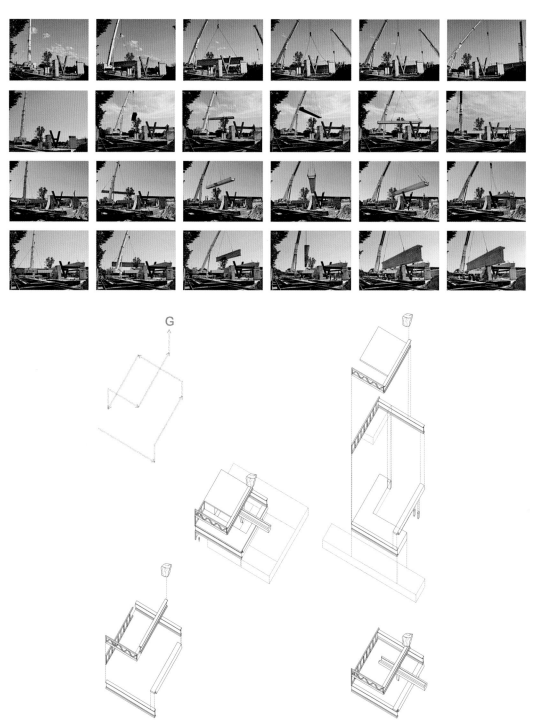

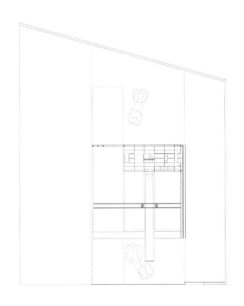

CASA HEMEROSCOPIUM. PLANTA COTA +3.07m.
HEMEROSCOPIUM HOUSE. PLAN LEVEL +3.07m.

Escala
Scale   0 1   5   10   20 m.

CASA HEMEROSCOPIUM. PLANTA COTA +6.52m.
HEMEROSCOPIUM HOUSE. PLAN LEVEL +6.52m.

Escala
Scale   0 1   5   10   20 m.

Matharoo Associates   **House with Balls**

2003–04
Ahmedabad, Gujarat,
India

Brutalist naked architecture in India is an imported product, and the memories of Le Corbusier and of Chandigarh echo in many buildings. Matharoo Associates designed this fascinating house built near Ahmedabad for the owner of an aquarium. The house extends longitudinally, opening its main façade towards the outside, while the rear is embedded delicately into the ground. The internal layout follows this longitudinal arrangement with a large living room along the full length, offset to the rear by a fish-tank. The idea of the large hanging concrete balls used as balances to open the steel shutters is simple but effective. A single material has been used in the construction of the house: reinforced concrete; essential, rough, archaic, bare.

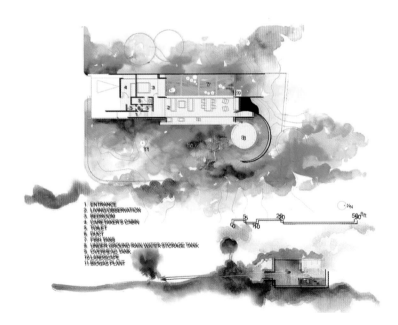

1 ENTRANCE
2 LIVING/OBSERVATION
3 BEDROOM
4 CARETAKER'S CABIN
5 TOILET
6 DUCT
7 FISH TANS
8 UNDER GROUND RAIN WATER STORAGE TANK
9 OVERHEAD TANK
10 LANDSCAPE
11 BIOGAS PLANT

Casa JD Vivienda de Veraneo

2006–09
Mar Azul, Buenos Aires,
Argentina

The house has an internal surface area of 150 square metres and stands on a slight slope, detaching itself from it in some specific areas. The building is divided into three levels: a semi-basement and two floors above ground. The first of these is cross-shaped, with the stairway at the centre, while the one above is set lengthwise and includes the main bedroom. The general configuration of the cross shape might recall Frank Lloyd Wright's Prairie House, but the appearance of this house is very different: rough and mildly brutal and essential in all its components. Some features of Naked Architecture are very evident: the almost total absence of any decoration, the external and internal identity of the materials and style of the building, as well as the typically brutal synthesis between structure and finish.

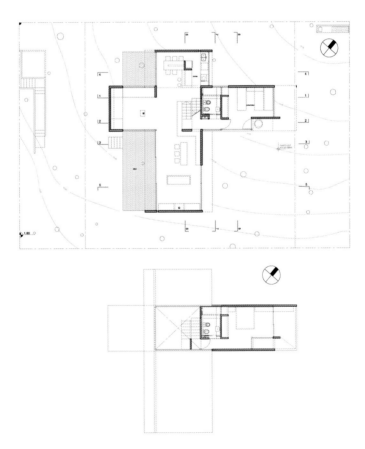

Cristián Undurraga   **Retreat Chapel**

2008–09
Valle de los Andes,
Chile

The volume of the chapel in the foothills of the Andes is formed of four high
concrete beams meeting to form a cross; the beams rest on eight plinths above
ground. From the outside, the chapel is of a rough, eloquent simplicity, like
a minimal sacred sculpture; the interior is instead more welcoming, being simply
panelled in wood, giving a sense of frugal cordiality.
The route down to the wholly inward-looking space of the chapel comes from
a ramp in the ground leading through a tunnel to what the architect wished
to be a room of light carved from the rock.

Drucker Arquitetura   **Makenna Resort**

2004–10
Ponta da Tulha, Bahia,
Brazil

In an area of great naturalistic interest to the south of Bahia, Drucker Arquitetura has designed a project that aims to attune itself to the place and fit in with it. The decision was taken to effect a basic architecture, based on a spare, naked modernism owing much to the Brazilian brutalist tradition of Niemeyer and Vilanova Artigas. The project consists of a clubhouse with restaurant and services surrounded by 16 bungalows over a total covered area of 6,700 square metres, the whole set into an area of 8 hectares facing the sea. The buildings are raised 70 cm off the ground to give the impression of being an ephemeral, reversible intervention, and the figurative connotation is founded on a horizontality contrasting with the vertical aspect of the surrounding palms.

LIVING AND RESTAURANT

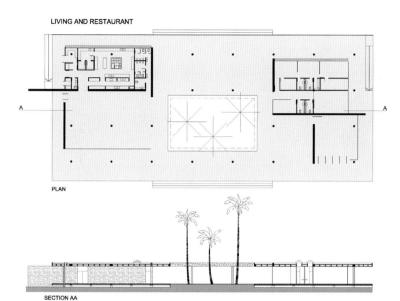

PLAN

SECTION AA

0 1 2 3 4 5   10   20

SPA

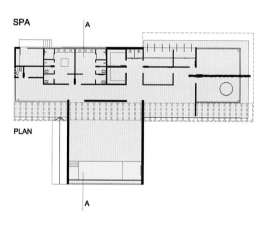

PLAN

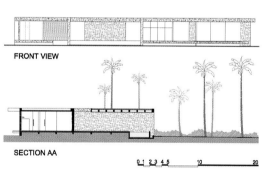

FRONT VIEW

SECTION AA

0 1 2 3 4 5   10   20

Kraanspoor Office Building

1997; 2006–07
Amsterdam, Netherlands

The large craneway (270 metres long, 13.50 metres high and 8.7 metres wide) was built in 1952 in the port of Amsterdam when this was undergoing a large expansion. Despite the industrial reconversion of recent decades, it was decided not to demolish the imposing structure, for which OTH has designed a building of three floors raised three metres from the extrados of the craneway. The new structure is laid asymmetrically to the one beneath as the foundations allowed for the greater load-barring function on the side of the ships, and this side is marked by a greater lightness. Two opposing types of nakedness are revealed in this building: the heavy, downward-bearing one of the old craneway and the light, airy one of the steel and glass structure by OTH.

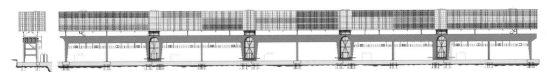

Façade - land side

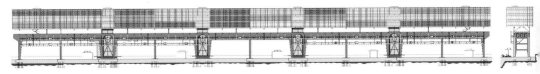

Façade - waterfront

cross section / longitudinal section

0m ———————— 25m

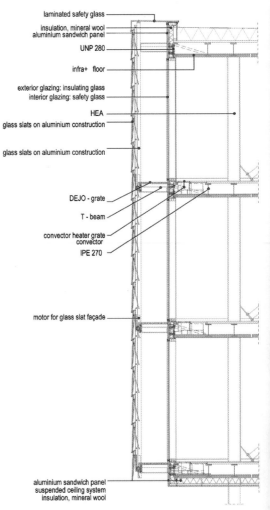

laminated safety glass

insulation, mineral wool
aluminium sandwich panel

UNP 280

infra+ floor

exterior glazing: insulating glass
interior glazing: safety glass

HEA

glass slats on aluminium construction

glass slats on aluminium construction

DEJO - grate

T - beam

convector heater grate
convector

IPE 270

motor for glass slat façade

aluminium sandwich panel
suspended ceiling system
insulation, mineral wool

Mestizo Restaurant

2005–07
Santiago, Chile

The project was the winning contribution in a competition for the construction of a restaurant at the edge of a park into which it was to be integrated as much as possible. The first solution planned by Radic was an ephemeral architecture. Over time, the project changed, rendering permanent that which had earlier been planned as temporary. On a slope, Radic placed a services block lengthwise from which radiate beams of reinforced concrete cast in situ in wooden formwork and then painted black. The procession of beams lies on a series of large granite boulders emerging from the floor. The result is a work combining the poetic of Richard Neutra's "getting away" with the archaic memory of menhirs.

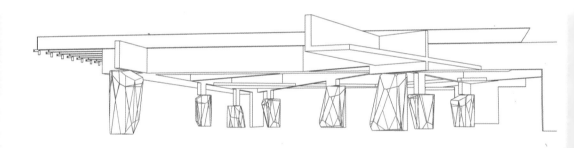

House in Ubatuba

2006–09
Ubatuba, Brazil

For this terrain sloping 45° down to the sea, Spbr presented a project whose aim was to touch the ground as little as possible. The building is divided into three blocks: one enters the upper floor from the road via a little bridge leading to a vast terrace housing the pool. From this terrace, one descends between the large empty spaces left by the volumes, which seem to be filled by the lush vegetation. The whole house is built of in situ concrete and built from the bottom upwards; in this regard, the top extrados beams that are essential for the static resistance of the building – since it is from these that hang the roof – came last.

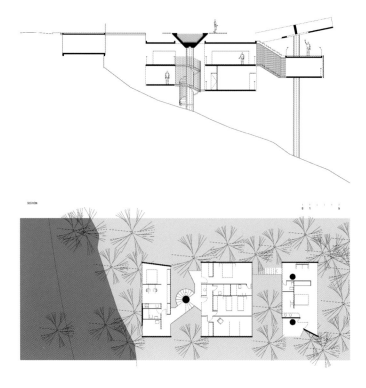

SECTION

LEVEL 74.00 / 74.90 / 75.90 - BEDROOMS

2008
Basel, Switzerland

The striking shape and size of the building result from the local building rules.
The project took part in the competion for the new building but was never built.
An important element in the structural design concept is the building corner
that cantilevers above the railway tracks and is suspended from a framework
incorporated into the building façade. This is balanced by a similar feature
at the diagonally opposite corner of the building.
This is achieved by incorporating structural suspension members into the façades
of the building, which in plan view run diagonally across the building in a straight
line, forming an H shape. This supports the loads of the building corners
at opposite ends, which are then diverted in the attic floor via diverter elements
and transferred to the main pillars and walls that form the core of the building.

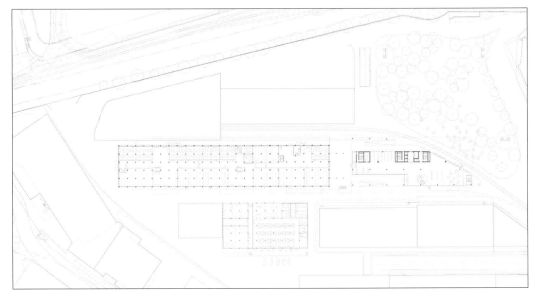

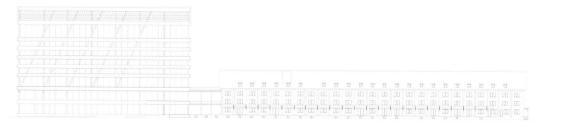

Bak Arquitectos

Concrete House in Mar Azul

2006–07
Mar Azul, Buenos Aires,
Argentina

This is a small holiday home (14 x 6.9 metres) designed by Bak Arquitectos in the pinewoods of Mar Azul near the ocean. The idea is that of a simple prism embedded in a slope declining transversally and longitudinally. It is the stereometric simplicity of the building that by contrast underlines the shape of the terrain, bringing the lesson of Land Art into architecture. The internal layout of the cottage presents a long porticoed front with beams and full-height windows set at intervals; behind these are the living room and bedroom. On the other longitudinal front, partly embedded in the ground, are the services. On this side, the vertical supports have been set back from the façade in order to enable a window running the entire length of the building. Only two materials are used in the house: exposed concrete and glass; the result is an architecture that appears like a crasis between the elementary nature of Giorgio Grassi and Aldo Rossi's architecture and the brutalism of the fifties.

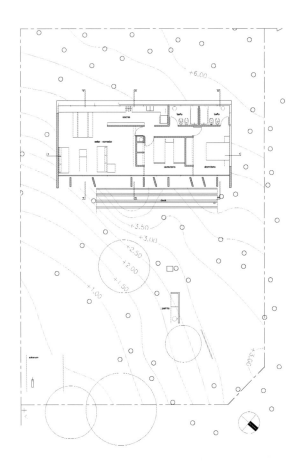

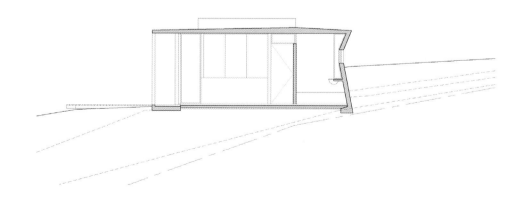

Thin Naked Architecture: an architecture that reduces the load-bearing sections as much as possible, which manipulates what is usual to obtain an unusual appearance. The Modern arose by challenging the notion that architecture should necessarily be a combination of mass, consistency and stability. The first attack on this notion came, as Hans Sedlmayr noted, via two trends of a strong symbolic significance: the severing of ties with the land and cantilevered construction, the corollary of which is the reduction of load-bearing sections to a minimum. One of the first projects to cause a reaction between the significance of cantilevered construction and that of slenderness was one for the central station for the Cité Industrielle (1901–04) by Tony Garnier, in which two slender and bare suspended floors emerge from the rigid central building and rest on equally slender and slightly flared pilasters. The inspiration clearly derived from naval origins, from the liners of the turn of the century, and from aircraft of the period; an inspiration that became the matrix for a new purist style under Le Corbusier. In the fifties, the architecture of the engineers would tend to concentrate on slenderness, especially in the roofs, panels and mushroom supports. In some cases, as in Candela, Nervi and, later, with Heinz Isler, an extreme slenderness is achieved but this was later rejected for reasons of cost and safety. From the seventies onwards, with the postmodern, slenderness not only lost its evocative capacity, but even became a negative value: its symbolism was forgotten in the name of a rediscovery of mass and *gravitas*. In recent times, we have witnessed a reversal of this trend: slenderness has regained its expressive context, although different to the past in that it is less bound to the three-dimensional structures and increasingly related to an iconic image of the whole architecture. Japanese architecture, which historically has tended towards the lightening of components,

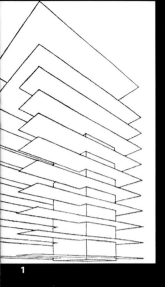

1

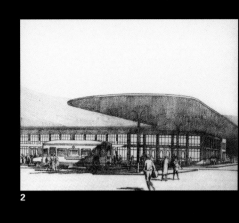

2

3

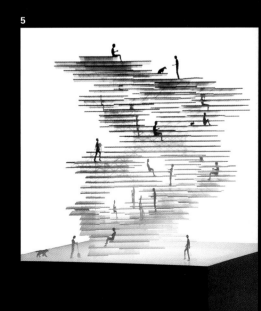

4

5

Angelo Bucci
Michael Braun
Ciro Miguel

House in Phoenix

2005
Phoenix, USA

For this semi-desert area marked by a harsh climate and great temperature range, the architects proposed a bare shell of a building in which the structural component, assured by engineering at the limit of anonymity, coincides with the image itself of the building. The house is laid out over three floors: on the ground floor, the layout is organic and follows the terrains with irregular spaces; the first floor, with a mesh of beams over an area of 40 square metres, includes the two volumes of the bedrooms, suspended from the roof; on the top floor, the ceilings over the rooms become panoramic terracing. The character of the project is that of a filigree-like nakedness, extremely thin and almost unreal.

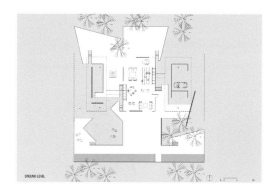

GROUND LEVEL

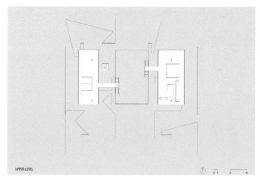

UPPER LEVEL

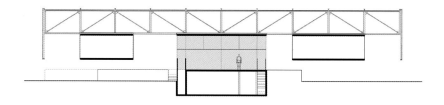

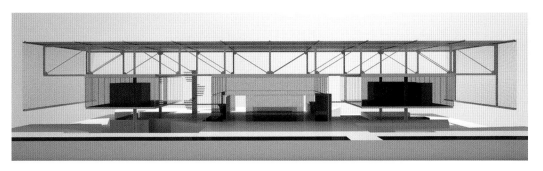

Akihisa Hirata   **Show Room H**

2005–06
Nigata, Japan

The exhibitions pavilion for agricultural equipment covers an area of almost 900 square metres and is organised over a square 5-metre grid rotated 45°.
The architect's intention was to create a continuous sense of space, in which one comes across objects exposed as though they were surprises. The nakedness of the extremely slender reinforced concrete beams and the angle of the openings in these, in line with a diagonal, amplify this sensation. In this work, we find a combination between echoes of the naked brutalist architecture of the fifties and sixties, and a wholly Japanese element of origami.

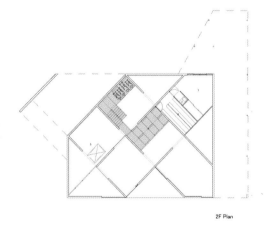

2F Plan

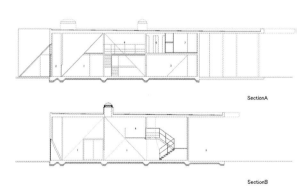

SectionA

SectionB

1. showroom   2. working space   3. office   4. loft   5. backyard   6.storage   7.rest room

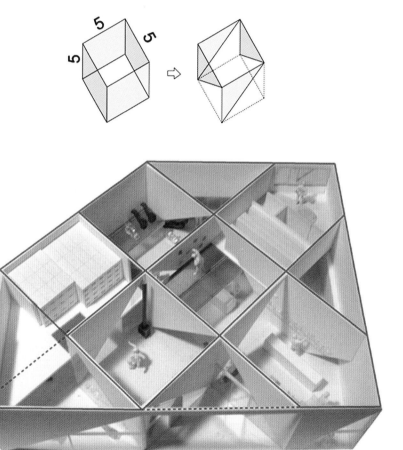

Tama Art University Library

2004–07
Hachiōji, Tokyo, Japan

This is one of the most successful examples of Naked Architecture: a range of variously sized arches, ranging from 2 to 16 metres, join in an arbitrary sequence determined in part by the functional requirements. The building has two floors above ground: the ground floor is totally bare to host campus events, while the upper floor houses the large reading room of the library; the basement floor is used as the book deposit for the library. The ground plan is a rectangle deformed at the corners, and the sequence of arches is made from a prefabricated steel structure covered with a thin layer of concrete in order to assure extreme slenderness. Albeit of an absolute clarity and essentialness, this project has a deliberately mannerist character about it: each element is modified artificially in such a way as to obtain a real transmutation from anonymity to extraordinariness.

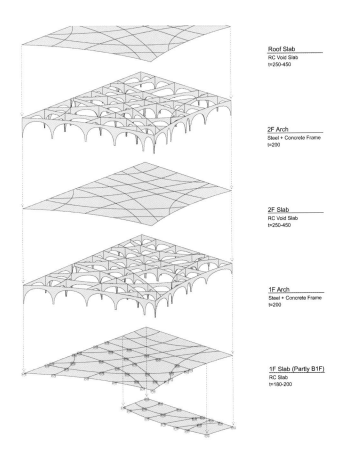

Roof Slab
RC Void Slab
t=250-450

2F Arch
Steel + Concrete Frame
t=200

2F Slab
RC Void Slab
t=250-450

1F Arch
Steel + Concrete Frame
t=200

1F Slab (Partly B1F)
RC Slab
t=180-200

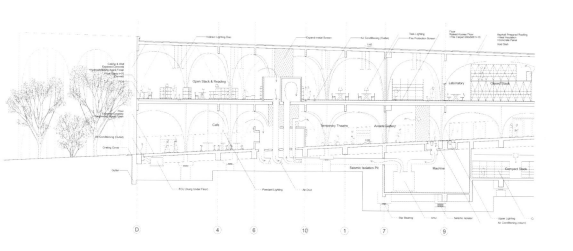

36 The Calls

2010
Leeds, United Kingdom

With this project, the architects intend to offer a modern revision of historic construction, in which the façade corresponds to the structural line of the building. The façade itself becomes a link between the sum of the vertical beams, agitated in their repeated rhythm, and the succession of horizontal slabs. This woven system deforms at ground level to open out into a public lobby, and at roof level, where it links the new project with the adjacent buildings. In its rhythmic nakedness, this project appears as an alternative to Gottfried Semper's theory of cladding that sharply divides the structural elements from the cladding ones; in this project by Fletcher Crane Architects, instead, the image of structure tends to coincide with that of cladding.

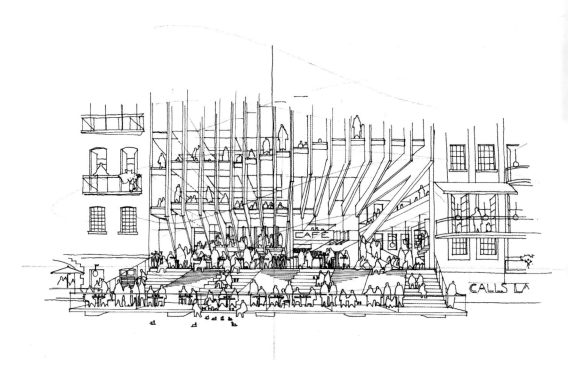

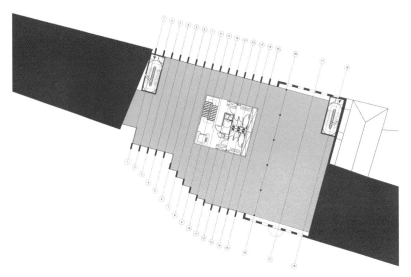

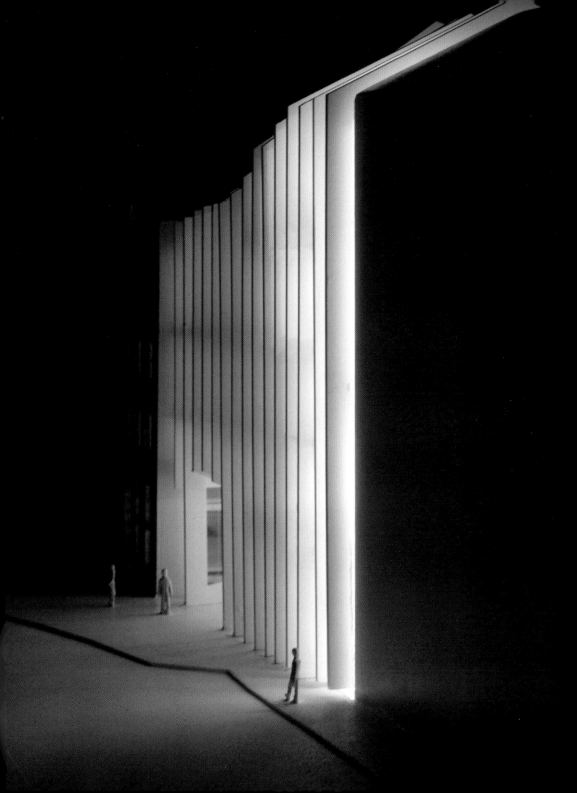

Aviary

2007–08
Parc "Bois-de-la-Bâtie",
Geneva, Switzerland

Thanks to their bold, innovative forms, two aviaries have entered the history books of modern architecture: one by Frei Otto at the Munich Zoo and the other by Cedric Price at London Zoo. Both cases present a naked and extremely light structure as architectural metaphors for the flight of birds. Group 8's aviary for the zoo in Geneva wishes to compare itself to these examples. The aviary is located on a small artificial island, and its organic form is determined by the need to preserve the nearby trees. The slender structure is formed of a very thin cement slab supported by steel columns like "bare trees", each different to the other. The designers' aim is that of "creating a very precise, fragile static equilibrium, like a bird on a small branch".

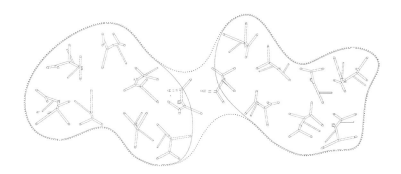

Mimosa Architekti   **Water House**

2010
Hulice,
Czech Republic

The role of this building is to celebrate the water resources of the place and
the associated ecosystems; for this reason, the slender architecture proposed
by Mimosa aims to be as crystal-clear like water as possible. The building should
be seen in relation to the surroundings, divided into various thematic areas,
each of which representing a biodiversity in the neighbourhood. These green
areas are crisscrossed by a network of paths that meet at the building, conceived
as a slender, almost impalpable flying roof. To increase the sense of the roof
levitating, the internal divisions are made of glass. The large space above ground
houses temporary exhibitions, while the basement houses the permanent
museum and services.

José María
Sánchez García

Footbridge across the River Drava

2010
Maribor, Slovenia

The project philosophy is explained in these terms by the architect: "The town already has a clear character which we did not wish to alter by adding an object with a strong impact. Our proposal was thus that of a new architectural feature for the river without image, without presence: an almost intangible structure, like a ghost bridge, like that of a tightrope walker on his rope. In this way, on some foggy days, it will seem that the bridge has almost vanished. And by night its 'absence' will mean that pedestrians and cyclists will feel as though they are suspended over the water". In order to achieve this intangible slenderness, the decision was taken to design a bridge coinciding with the form of trusses that have been made very high in order to be as slender as possible; so high, indeed, that there are three levels to the bridge. The 130-metre long truss is supported only at the ends and has no buttresses in the river itself.

PHASE 1   PHASE 2   PHASE 3

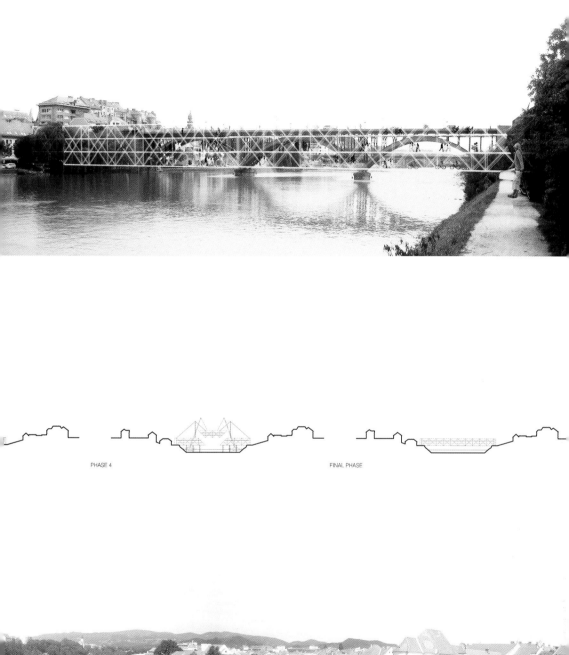

PHASE 4

FINAL PHASE

Nivo 3_GLAVNI TRG (nivo centra mesta) 265,2m.

Nivo 1_ LENT-TABOR
(nivo reke) 256,7m.

Nivo 3_GLAVNI TRG (nivo centra mesta) 265,2m.

Nivo 1_LENT-TABOR
(nivo reke) 256,7m.

DRAVA

Junya Ishigami   **Kanagawa Institute of Technology – KAIT**

2007–10
Kanagawa, Japan

This building consists of a thicket of 305 slender steel columns disposed
in arbitrary fashion like the stars in a constellation. The columns are 5 metres high
and support a steel caisson with skylights along the full length. Along the ground,
there is a uniform cement floor outlining a base of 47 by 46 metres. The result
is of an absolute simplicity, and yet attaining this simplicity has only been made
possible through engineering able to take the thinness of the elements
to their extreme. Ishigami states: "I wanted to make a space with very ambiguous
borderlines, which has a fluctuation between local spaces and the overall space,
rather than a universal space like that of Mies. This allows a new flexibility
to emerge, revealing reality rather than shaping it".

Nube Arena

2010
Las Torres de Cotillas,
Spain

The proposal by Sou Fujimoto for the international competition for an auditorium aims to offer an extreme, allegorical and dreamlike image. The whole effect is founded on a ramp that rises upwards like a spiral, seemingly weightless and unreal, as though made of smoke. This simple but extreme project brings to mind the words of Novalis: "In giving a high meaning to the ordinary, a mysterious aspect to what is everyday, the dignity of the unknown to the known, an infinite appearance to the finite, I make them romantic".

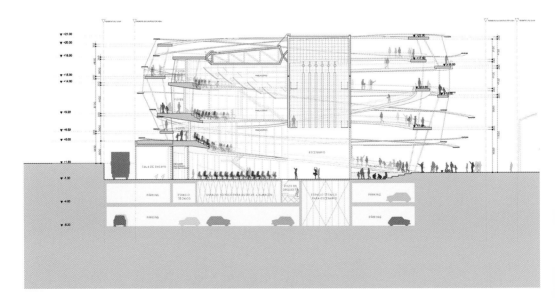

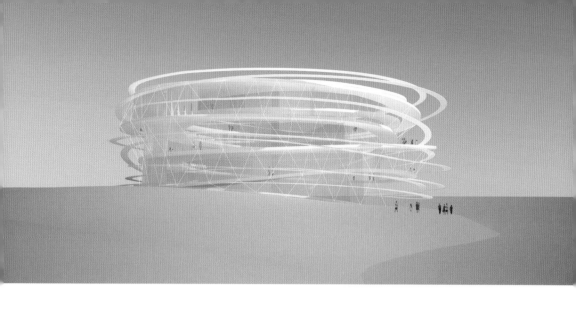

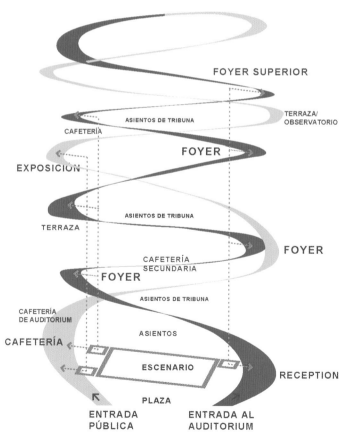

FOYER SUPERIOR

TERRAZA/
OBSERVATORIO

ASIENTOS DE TRIBUNA

CAFETERÍA

FOYER

EXPOSICIÓN

ASIENTOS DE TRIBUNA

TERRAZA

FOYER

CAFETERÍA
SECUNDARIA

FOYER

ASIENTOS DE TRIBUNA

CAFETERÍA
DE AUDITORIUM

ASIENTOS

CAFETERÍA

ESCENARIO

RECEPTION

PLAZA

ENTRADA
PÚBLICA

ENTRADA AL
AUDITORIUM

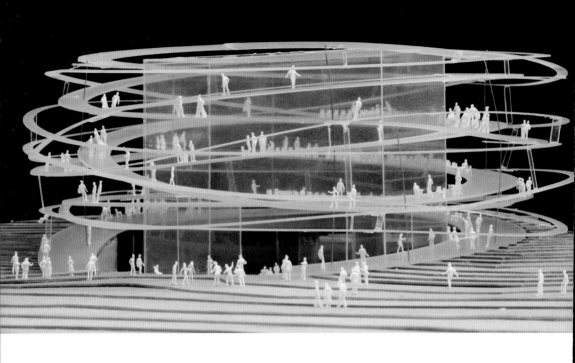

174

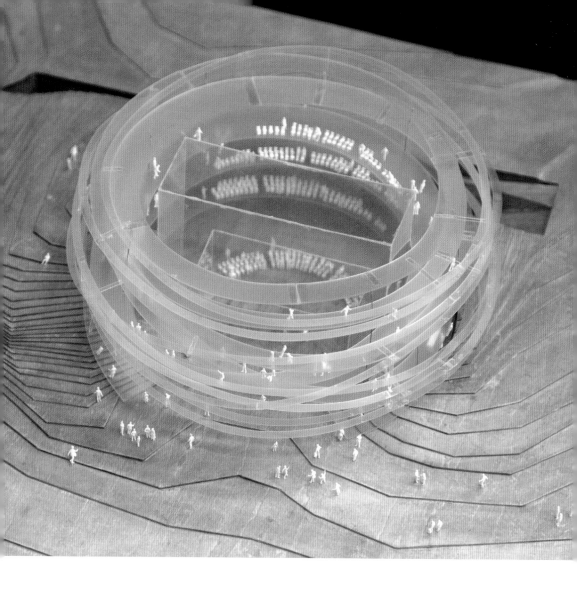

Lyric

Lyrical Naked Architecture: a naked, lyrical, evocative and terse architecture, at times even fairytale-like. In the early fourties, the Futurist painter Enrico Prampolini presented some projects comprising a single summary line enclosing a terse, abstract and naked surface.These projects were the result of work undertaken by the artist over decades on what he called "bioplastic architecture": an atmospheric architecture based on a lyrical and vaguely surreal dynamism, held together by what Filippo Tommaso Marinetti had defined as "the unique line". The most effective example of bioplastic architecture is without a doubt the Breda Pavilion at the Fiera di Milano (1952) by Luciano Baldessari in which the line acquires a lightness evoking a baroque festoon. A few years earlier, in his architectural visions, Hans Scharoun had offered his own expressionistic interpretation of the intuitions of the Italian Futurists. Probably the only architect to have founded his entire poetics on lyrical nudity is Oscar Niemeyer, who saw in Le Corbusier's sketches of the thirties a sense of architecture finally emancipated of the right angle and volumetric contraction, and who gave rise to an architecture made of line, summary, one that was both essential and expansive. The influence of the architecture of the engineers of the fifties has been influential in naked lyrical architecture too. Until the advent of post-modern historicism, which cancelled out this trend, it is possible to find some works that in different ways express the sense of a lyrical nudity. An example that is unusual – in that it is in some way kitsch – is the design by Angelo Mangiarotti for a wind tunnel for cars (1961). In general, the sense of lyrical nudity can be understood through two parameters. The first is explained in the words of Lord Kames who in the mid-18th century wished for an architecture that had the capacity to seize the mind with such a summary impression as to reduce itself "to a single blow". This component is joined by a dreamlike one, appropriately described by Jun Hashimoto and Jun Aoki when they speak of "architectural ghosts", of summary architecture, of light but impalpable forms, able to give the impression of being on the point of vanishing.

1. Luciano Baldessari
Breda Pavilion at the Fiera
di Milano, 1952
2. Hans Scharoun
Architectural fantasy,
1939–45, watercolour
3. Oscar Niemeyer
Museum of
Contemporary Art, 1996
Niterói, Brazil

4. Félix Candela
Structure on lake
Tequesquitengo, 1957
Morelos, Mexico
5. Angelo Mangiarotti
Project for wind tunnel
for testing cars, 1961

1

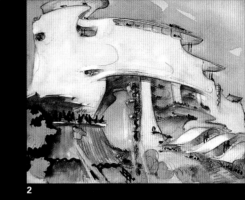

2

3

5

4

SANAA
Kazuyo Sejima
+ Ryue Nishizawa

Rolex Learning Center

2005–10
Lausanne, Switzerland

For the École Polytechnique Fédérale de Lausanne, SANAA designed a dreamlike building: two slabs of like form lie softly on the ground, like a rug in the instant before falling to the ground. These two slabs (which frame a space within of 20,000 square metres) are pierced by a series of holes of varying sizes configuring some patios. At the centre of the building, one arrives at a uniform, soft orographic space, like a scene from some science-fiction movie. There are no stairs in the building and the supports between the two slabs are reduced to a minimum. The structural solution and engineering of the Rolex Centre is the work of one of the most renowned engineers around today: Mutsuro Sasaki, who has been working on *flux structures* for years: a plastic evolution of the catenary arches and thin shells anticipated by Antoni Gaudí and Heinz Isler.

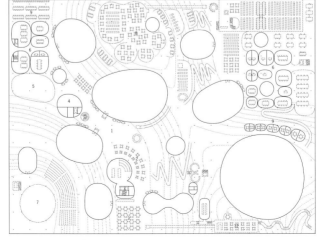

1 Main entrance
2 Cafe
3 Food court
4 Bank
5 Bookshop
6 Offices
7 Multipurpose hall
8 Library
9 Work area
10 Ancient books collection
11 Research collection
12 Restaurant

Floor plan   10m

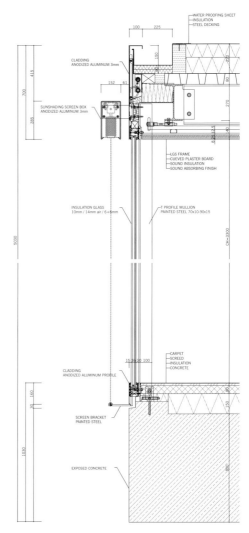

Typical facade section

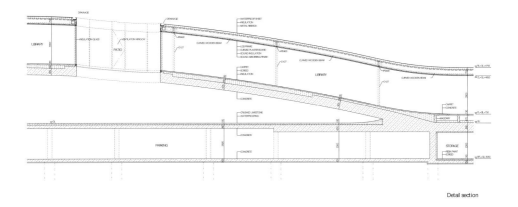

Detail section

Patkau Architects   **Our Lady of the Assumption Parish Church**

2008
Port Coquitlam,
Vancouver, Canada

The project for the church, planned for a Vancouver suburb, comprises two spaces: the nave, with room for 700 worshippers, and the chapel for 300. The two spaces can be easily combined into a single one. The church summarises the official liturgy in a form whose outline recalls that of the intrados of a cave. The idea is that of a slender pleated wall, divided into a sequence of beams in the ceiling that remind of Luigi Moretti's theoretical studies on interior space. The wall is formed of a sandwich of metal plates within which runs the load-bearing structure, itself of steel.

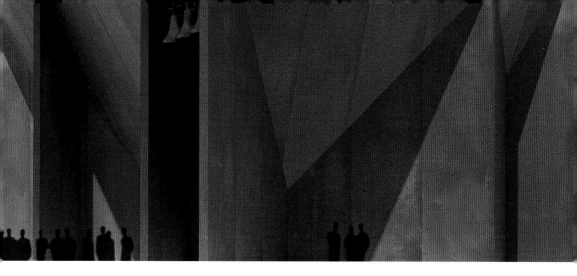

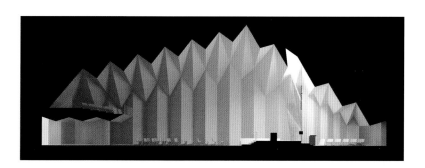

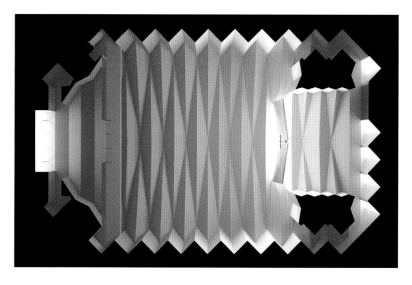

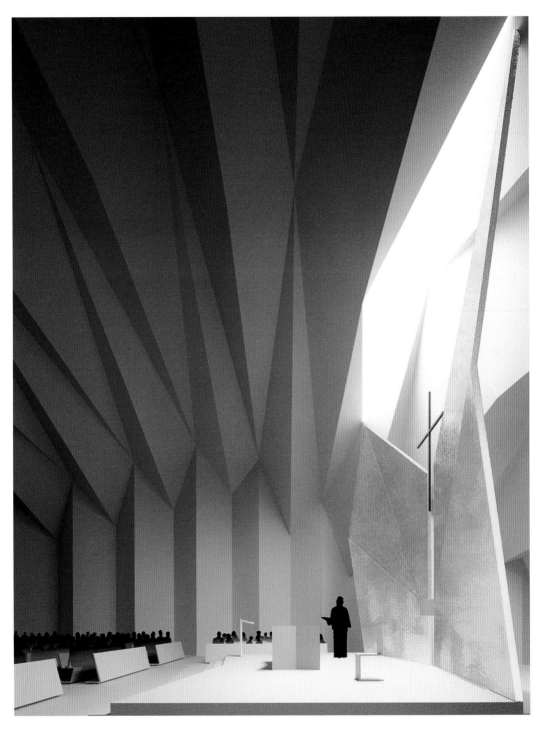

Guillermo Vázquez
Consuegra

Medina Museums Complex

2008
Medina, Saudi Arabia

The complex designed by Consuegra is the result of an overlay of a series
of circles corresponding to large empty spaces over a wide, low horizontal slab
at the centre of which there is a covered piazza, conceived as the project's centre
of gravity. The result is a megastructure of walls, of pure continuous space;
a metaphor, the architect intends, for the cities of northern Africa. From
an iconographic point of view, the reference to the Arab figurative culture,
iconoclastic and calligraphic, is evident, but tending towards a nakedness whose
meaning is intimately religious. In this project, the Naked Architecture express
itself through a system of basic walls enveloping a bare, plastic space,
and appearing in the play of light and shade transcribed to the walls themselves.

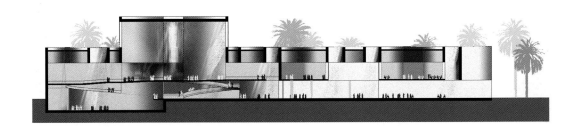

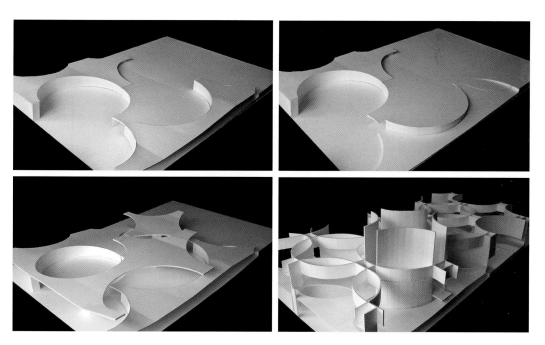

Christian Kerez   **Museum of Modern Art**

2007
Warsaw, Poland

This project won an international competition and is part of a vast refurbishment programme for the centre of Warsaw. The L-shaped building appears of an absolute compactness from the outside: blind walls serving as beams contain the rhythmic surges of a varied series of waves of roofing identifying the different rooms; these rooms are lit from above via a system of skylights. All that appears in this project is a series of monochromatic walls and beams of a single material. The result is an architecture that intentionally forms a backdrop and is conceived in such a way as to create a number of relaxing but figuratively distinctive spaces.

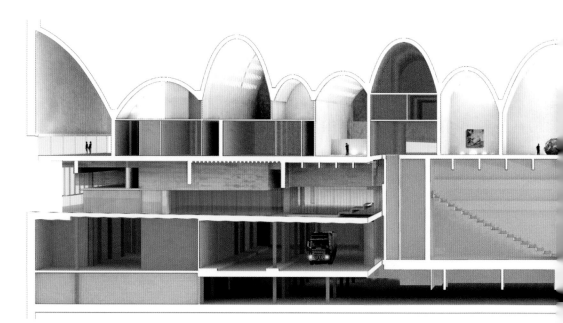

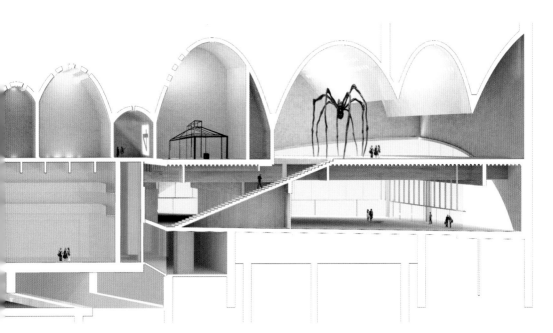

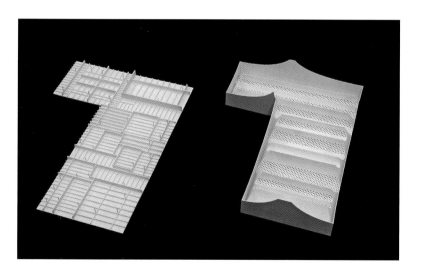

Valerio Olgiati

Perm Museum XXI

2008
Perm, Russia

The museum has a fairy-tale-like appearance: a 57-metre tower formed
of an overlay of slabs woven together by the repetition of a pattern of strong
visual impact and which also has a structural function as a continuous side beam.
The entire construction (façades, floors and walls) is of white cement cast on-site.
The project is characterised by an extremely concise structural solution: a hollow
central nucleus is the soul of the project, housing the lifts, emergency stairs,
skylights and lavatories; the floors emerge from this nucleus via four full-height
consoles. As regards the internal layout, the lobby is on the ground floor, and from
here one can climb to the foyer on the floor above or descend to the auditorium
on the floor beneath. The upper floors house exhibition spaces, with the last
floors reserved for restaurants and panoramic areas.

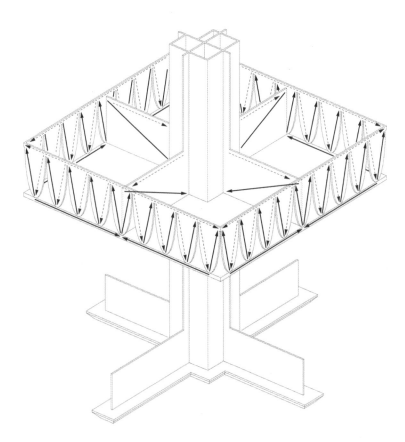

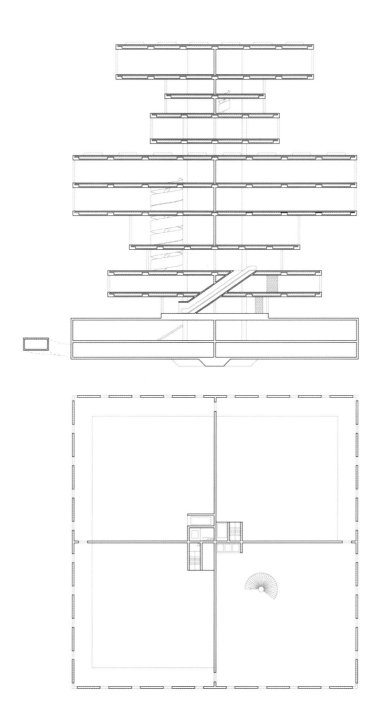

Aires Mateus Associados
Antonio Tejedor Cabrera

Atrium of the Alhambra

2011
Cordoba, Spain

The project takes the form of an elementary prism slotting into a slope
in the ground in a figure that owes much to Land Art and the dialectic contrasts
between natural softness and the hardness of basic geometric forms. This as far
as the outward appearance is concerned; the interior instead offers a succession
of ancestral spaces, some with vaulting, others without, lit from above.
Rather than describing it in terms of tectonics or textile arts, it is more accurate
here to speak of stereotomy, a configuration that harks back to the stone
construction with a transport of romanticism. The result is a building that aspires
to be timeless: at once modern and archaic, and in which persists the romantic
memory of Chtonic architecture and of its ruins.

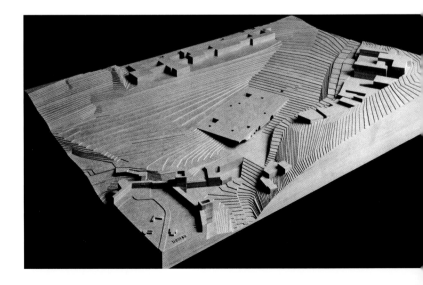

206

Mansilla + Tuñón
Arquitectos

Museum of Cantabria

2003
Vaguada de las Llamas,
Santander, Spain

The architects declare: "The project for the Museum of Cantabria intends to build an artificial geography, a forest of mountains". The ground plan is formed of a network of irregular trapeziums that configure a sequence of half-enclosed spaces within the complex. This organisation of the plan emerges above ground in a jungle of large and crooked pyramid-shaped skylights, broken off irregularly. The general image imposes with its presence that seems to manipulate the Naked Architecture to achieve an image offering a strong lyrical and metaphorical impact, a stylization of an ancestral, timeless landscape owing much to symbolist iconography but also to science-fiction strip cartoons.

TORRE CERREDO

NARANJO DE BULNES

TORRE DE LA CELADA

PICO TESORERO

TORRE DE LA PALANCA

CUCHALLÓN

TORRE DE LLANBRION

TORRE LLAGO

TORRE BERMEJA

TORRE BLANCA

PEÑA VIEJA

MADEJUNO

TORRE SALINAS

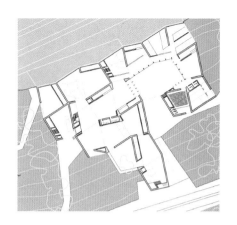

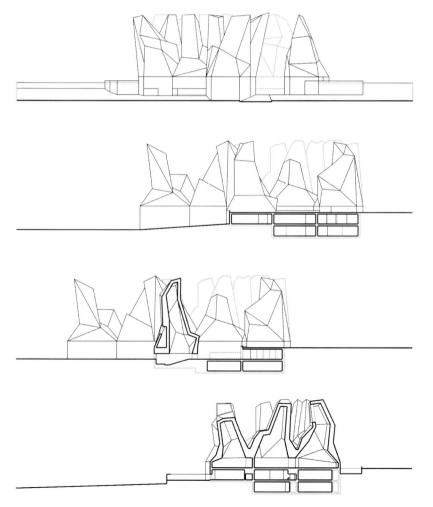

Ryue Nishizawa
Rei Naito

Teshima Art Museum

2004–10
Teshima Island, Japan

In issue 67 of *Japan Architecture*, an article speaks of "spatial ghosts" of a strong visual impact yet evanescent, fleeting, ready to dissolve like the Cheshire Cat in *Alice in Wonderland*. The museum, built to house the works of sculptor Rei Naito, is the paradigmatic example of this naked, evanescent architecture, an almost nothing that seems a dream or fairy tale.
The museum is located on a hill on the island of Teshima. Its form intends to be the architectural transposition of a drop of water on a table, in like manner to the works of art by Naito within the building. This drop is built from a slender shell of white cement covering a space of 40 by 60 metres. In the ceiling (4.5 metres high), whose complete whiteness blends with the floor, there are two large holes framing the sky. In this case, we may speak of a sidereal, atmospheric nakedness.

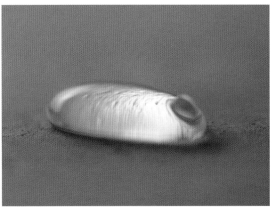
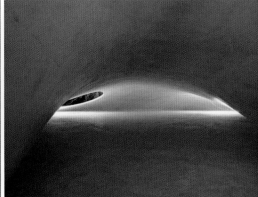

Maribor Gallery

2010
Maribor, Slovenia

The project for this museum on the riverbank aims to be the metaphorical
apparition of an abstract forest of columns dotting a continuous space.
The chalice-shaped pillars immediately recall Frank Lloyd Wright's Johnson Wax
Administration Building, although in this case they appear to have undergone
a drastic stylization. Through its Eden-like appearance, the project should be seen
as being similar in approach to the research developed over years by Andrea
Branzi into what he calls "weak and widespread utopias": images and settings
alluding to a return to a simplification of forms and lifestyles able to reconquer
a desired collective innocence, stripped of today's sophistications.

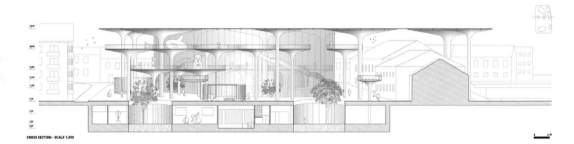

CROSS SECTION - SCALE 1:200

BIG
Bjarke Ingels Group

National Gallery of Greenland

2010
Nuuk, Greenland

This project by BIG is paradigmatic of naked lyricism. The building is extremely simple: a compact ring resting on the topography changes with it as though it were soft, giving the impression of an archaic construction whose foundations have subsided with the years. As in the case of bio-plastic Futurist architecture, there is a single style and the perception one has of this object is so synthetic that one needs only see a fragment to understand the whole. In the 18th century, Lord Kames and Winckelmann had written of an architecture that, fully perceived at first glance, would take on a magnificence able to evoke the sublime.
This idea recurs in BIG's project in a Pop key.

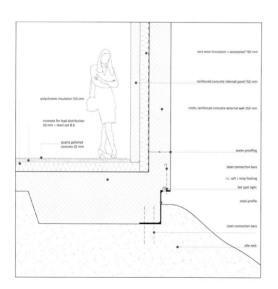

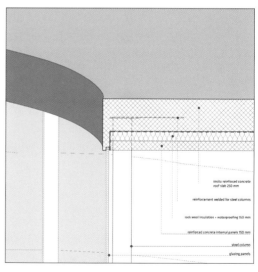

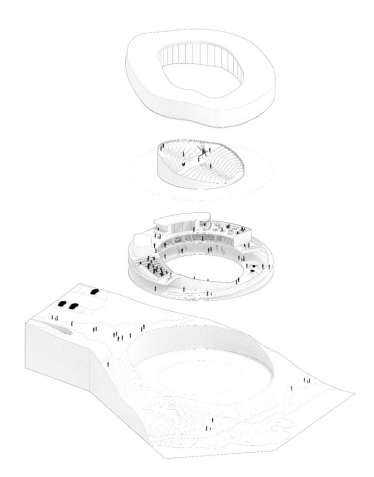

Frugal Naked Architecture: a humble architecture tending towards the rustic and establishing an equilibrium between structure and cladding. The Modern style has had a humble, frugal tradition that runs parallel to an eloquent and abstract one. A few years before Walter Gropius designed the skyscraper for the Herald Tribune or the Bauhaus, he designed the Sommerfeld House with Adolf Meier (1920–21), a picturesque work, in which the elements of construction were left exposed in rustic fashion. The spirit of humble architecture in the West looks back to the tradition of Christian art and the allegorical realism of Giotto and Dürer. The theoretical codification of frugal architecture in the modern sense was effected by Gottfried Semper, who in 1851 countered Laugier's rustic hut with a more controversial Caribbean hut in which a cladding is not denied, indeed, through the form of the wall, it is considered its founding aspect. The result was an architecture which, despite not denying a cladding, appeared humble and frugal. This interpretation became clearer to a greater extent many years later with Le Corbusier when, for his design for his Weekend Home (1935), he declared that his aim was to design an architecture in which all that was to be visible were the elements of the rustic construction, a principle that became a paradigm with the project for the Maisons Murondins (1940). In those same years, Frank Lloyd Wright in the United States was, with the Usonian Houses, suggesting an organic interpretation of frugality, which seemed to seek a dialogue with the origins of North American culture. This concept in the United States passed from the rustic organicism of Wright in the early fifties to steel and glass modernism. Such is the case with the Case Study Houses, dominated by what is called *cheap space* although rich in comfort. This is especially clear in one work by Paul Rudolph, the Finney Guest House (1947). In the name of sustainability, we are today witnessing an important return of frugal architecture. In some cases, such as in the Rural Studio, this concept becomes a life style and didactic approach.

1. Albrecht Dürer
Engraving from *Life of the Virgin*, 1501–02
2. Gottfried Semper
Layout of a Caribbean hut,

4. Paul Rudolph
Finney Guest House, 1947
Siesta Key, USA
5. Samuel Mockbee
(Rural Studio)

1

2

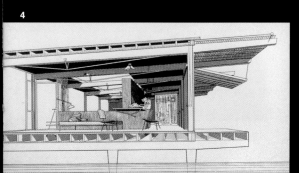

3

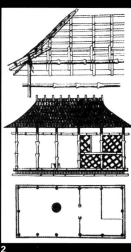

4

5

Mountain House

2008
Mother Lode,
California, USA

The Mountain House was the first construction to be built by the Atelier Bow-Wow in the United States, and is located in the Sierra Nevada in California. The natural setting is highly unusual and appealing, being marked by the traces of the explosions set off during the 19th-century gold rush. The two Japanese designers present an extremely simple and compact cabin set into a slope, in which the space on the lower floor supports a wooden terrace protected by a crooked roof that looks out like a beak over the landscape. The base of the house is made using prefabricated panels, while the upper part is a naked structure in rough timber from the sawmills near the house. The poetic of the Atelier Bow-Wow is clear in this work: domestic frugality, essential construction and the stressing of forms and materials drawn from the vernacular building style.

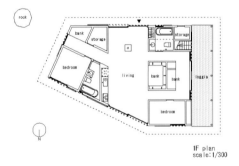

IF plan
scale:1/300

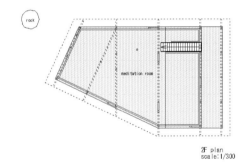

2F plan
scale:1/300

section
scale:1/300

Alter Smith
Michel Bazantay

Nine Wood Frame Houses

2008
Vouneuil-sous-Biard,
France

The structure of these nine houses is extremely simple and economical: panels, beams and pilasters of wood are composed in accordance with a logic at the limits of anonymity. Equally anonymous is the functional layout, with a blind north front housing garage and barn, while the south front opens out in a full-height portico. The day area looks out on to this area, with the night-time area on the floor above. The double-height portico and translucent cladding walls provide for a winter garden that can be opened in the summer. The frugal and ecological nakedness that is to be found in some of the most interesting French architects, especially Lacaton & Vassal, is very evident here.

José María Sánchez
García

Sports Centre

2006–08
Guijo de Granadilla,
Cáceres, Spain

For a small peninsula of the reservoir behind a dam on the river Tago,
José María Sánchez García has designed a project of absolute clarity: a crown
with a cross-section measuring 7 by 4.2 metres describing a circle of 200 metres
diameter. The "constructed circle" is raised 6 metres above the ground as
protection against flooding. On the ground floor, solid areas alternate with empty
ones from which rise the slender piers supporting the structure above. The plan
is of an astonishing simplicity, and the technology used is equally simple: steel
and glass in their humblest forms used with such extreme essentialness
as to recall Pierre Koenig's Case Study Houses. Throughout the project,
the relationship between structure and cladding is clear, with the latter made
from alternating panels of chrome-plated metal sheeting or glass.

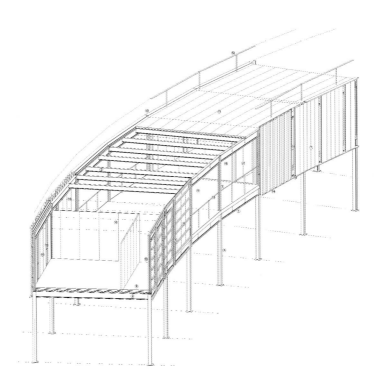

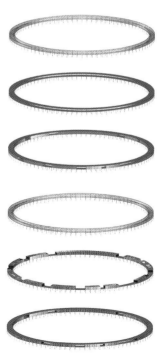

Anne Lacaton
& Jean-Philippe Vassal

School of Architecture

2009
Nantes, France

Three decks 9, 16 and 22 metres from the ground are served by a ramp that
progressively brings the road beneath into contact with the terrace overhead.
An extremely light metallic structure characterises the interior of a building with
a clear layout which intends to be as anonymous as possible. The interior, marked
by a naked, underlying sobriety, is left as much as possible in a state that enables
it to be colonised by the daily activities of the students. The architects' intention
is to strip the building as much as possible to give life to what they call an
architecture able to call itself a "didactic instrument". For years, Lacaton & Vassal
have been working towards an architecture reduced to bare essentials; a residual
one, even, adaptable to requirements. It is they who designed one of the clearest
and strictest interpretations of Naked Architecture conceived as an instrument
for assuring a frugality that is not only functional but aesthetic too.

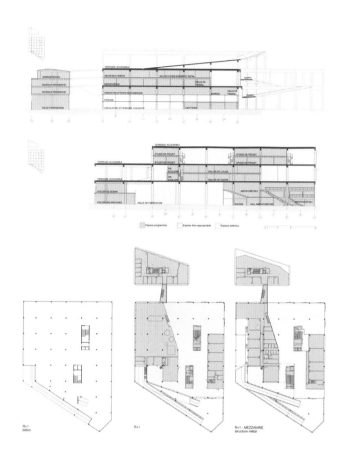

Studio Mumbai   **Palmyra House**

2005–07
Nandgaon,
Maharashtra, India

Two box-like constructions set at a slight angle to each other give life to a form of architecture that appears as a transposition of the model of the Caribbean hut by Gottfried Semper, with the distinction effected by Semper between stereotomic features (linked to the ground, such as the base and the fireplace) and the tectonic ones (conceived on the binding features, such as the structure and light, interwoven cladding). In other words, one might affirm that in this house by Studio Mumbai, the primary elements of the construction, structure and cladding find a frugal and serene balance.

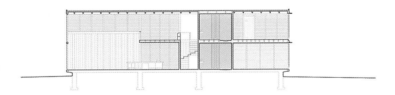

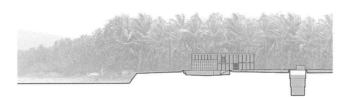

Women's Health Centre "G. Kambou"

2007
Ouagadougou,
Burkina Faso

The Centre"G. Kambou" is formed of a reinforced concrete platform raised above
the ground, on which stand two small single-storey buildings (250 square metres
each) built of rough bricks laid without cement. The roof of these buildings has
a steel structure and cladding of alternating strips of corrugated metal and others
of translucent corrugated PVC, which let in the light.
Above the pavilions, supported by galvanised steel tree-shaped columns,
a PVC sail protects the buildings and spaces around them from the sun.
The project's spirit is clearly expressed by the architects: "Every compositional
element has been planned as ideologically and physically separated from
the others, in order to maximise the possibility of reconfiguring the layout
and expandability of the system, as well as its architectural legibility".

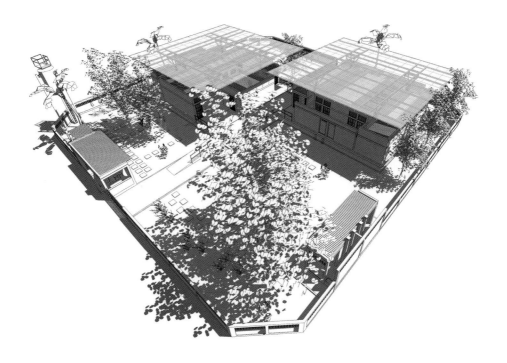

Carlos Castanheira
& Clara Bastai

Adpropeixe House

2005–08
Terras de Bouro, Gerês,
Portugal

The house, covering an area of about 200 square metres, stands in an attractive nature reserve. Construction was made possible following the demolition of a preceding and larger building. In terms of general layout, materials and techniques adopted, there is nothing invented in this work; everything has been redesigned in conformity with a sensitivity aiming to render evident any moment of the construction process. The use of wood recalls that of Frank Lloyd Wright's Usonian Houses, and the sense of frugality the house emanates recalls the best vernacular American architecture. In general, this house highlights the potential of a style of architecture that chooses to keep to the traditional language and construction techniques, and deliberately rejects design from the domestic space.

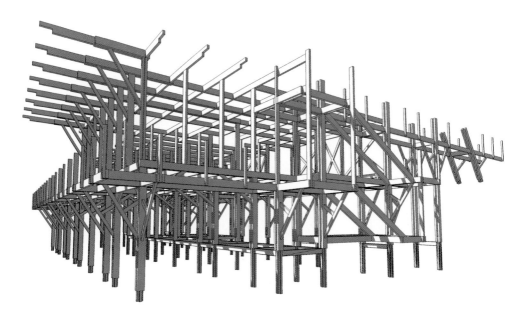

Luis Aldrete

Pilgrims Refuge

2010
Jalisco, Mexico

A wholly Spartan, naked architecture designed to give momentary refuge for pilgrims. It consists of a rectangular building which in layout makes use of divisions laid out in a form that recalls Alvar Aalto. But while the layout is the result of a modern composition, the upper floor is wholly different, being rustic and rural in feel. The pattern of light ochre-coloured bricks, of a sort used locally, is of fundamental importance for determining the image of the building: all it takes is the elegant pattern and how this varies in the different parts of this small building to determine its image and character.

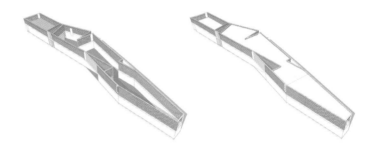

Ataria Visitors' Centre

2001–08
Vitoria, Spain

Near a small town in north-eastern Spain, not far from the houses, there are
some wetlands of great significance for which QVE Arquitectos has designed
a visitors' centre of great simplicity. A series of longitudinal elements emerge
towards the river forming a viewpoint overhanging the torrent beneath.
The structure has reinforced concrete and steel foundations, whilst the part above
ground is almost all of wood. The 2000 square metre interior is very similar
to the exterior, and is marked by the sequence of wooden structures.
Decorative features are reduced to minimum throughout, in order to give
as much impression of a frugal construction as possible but not minimal.

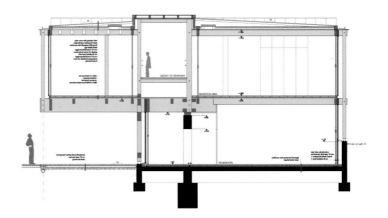

Primitive Naked Architecture: an archaic, archetypical form the aim of which is to appear timeless. Nakedness in architecture has always harked back to the archaic and primitive, but the birth of naked architecture as we know it can be attributed to the publication of the Laugier treatise, whose frontispiece portrays the famous rustic hut, the expression of an ideal, primitive and uncorrupted state in which nature and reason were to combine in harmony, as Rousseau would have expected. Laugier declared: "The little primitive hut I have just described constitutes the model from which every architectural magnificence has been conceived, and only by approximating the simplicity of this first model in practice and art will it be possible to avoid defects and attain genuine perfection". Laugier translated into his architectural image a spirit of the times that was increasingly attracted by the primitive. Successively, this feeling was transformed into an ethical paradigm of an aesthetic nature. Once again, it was Le Corbusier who established the need to give life to an architecture of primitive immediacy, taking archaic constructions as a model. The idea, borrowed from Loos, is that by placing truths and the skills of engineers in reaction together, a definitively true, spontaneous and objective architecture would spring to life. What is striking in primitive nakedness is its constant success. This is especially true in art, through a continuous line running from Picasso to Basquiat and on to the present day. The same success can be seen in architecture, although the sense of the primitive has been relegated most times to architecture of reduced dimensions.

Today, in parallel with frugal architecture, naked primitive architecture is undergoing a period of strong development that has enabled it to make a leap forward in terms of size: no longer just shelters and huts, but entire and complex buildings. Moreover, the significance and taste for the primitive increasingly tends towards an explicit expressiveness, as though it had definitively emancipated itself of the moral implications of Laugier's primitive hut. Giorgio Agamben's words are significant in this regard: "Historians of architecture and art know that between the archaic and modern there is a secret appointment [...] and this because the key to the modern is hidden in the immemorial and prehistoric".

1. Spontaneous architecture in Africa, from Christian Norberg-Schulz, *Genius Loci. Towards a Phenomenology of Architecture*, 1979

2. Marc-Antoine Laugier *Essai sur l'Architecture* Frontispiece to the 1755 edition
3. Le Corbusier Layout of a primitive temple, from *Vers une architecture*, 1923

4. John Lautner Refuge in the desert, 1937
5. Antón García-Abril Headquarters of the society of authors and publishers, 2004 Santiago de Compostela, Spain

1

2

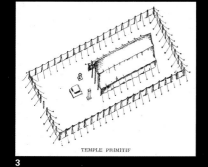

TEMPLE PRIMITIF

3

4

5

Antón García-Abril   **La Trufa**

2006–10
Costa da Morte,
Spain

La Trufa (The Truffle) is an archaic, dreamlike, ancestral apparition more than a
house. The construction method is very unusual: "We made a hole in the ground
and heaped the earth around the edge of the hole to create a containment dam
[…]. Then we built a volume using bales of hay heaped on to each other and then
poured concrete over these. After this, we removed the earth and uncovered
an amorphous mass. The earth and cement exchanged their properties […].
Then we effected some cuts to explore its central point and revealed the internal
mass made of hay, compressed by the hydrostatic pressure exercised by the
concrete on the fragile grassy structure. To empty the interior, we used a calf,
Paulina, who enjoyed 50 cubic metres of good food […]. After having digested
the internal volume, the space was revealed".

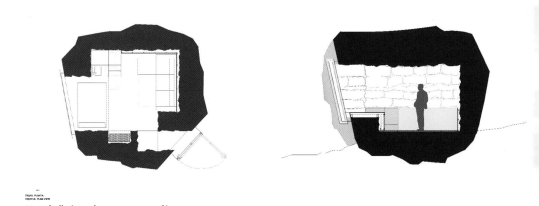

TRUFA. PLANTA
TRUFFLE. PLAN VIEW

Escala   0   0,5   1   2   5 m.
Scale

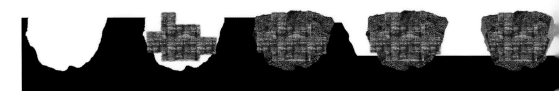

Monovolume

Tschapit Bridge

2001
Alpe di Siusi,
Bolzano, Italy

The Tschapit bridge is based on the typical Alpine method of construction using wood, and marks the passage between the uncontaminated Alpine environment and the tourist huts of the Sciliar Nature Reserve. Just two materials are used in the construction: the load-bearing structure is round larch, which is resistant to all the atmospheric elements, and these are bound together using steel elements. Tree trunks set at a tangent to each other form two parallel arches linked by beams. The railing is made using galvanised steel cables set in a ray pattern. The use of local untreated timber conveys natural characteristics to the structure which fit into the Alpine surroundings in a sensitive manner. The details are simple and clear and the construction is reduced to the minimum requirements.

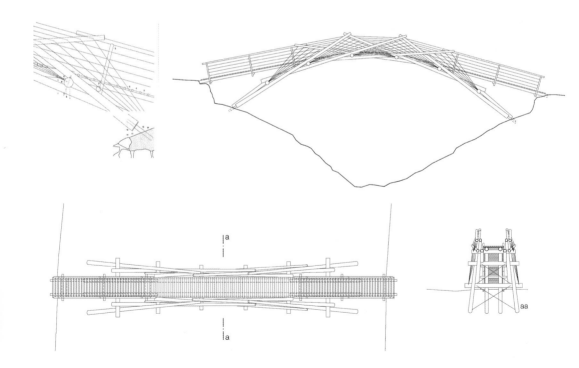

Children Education Center

2007–09
Koh Kood, Thailand

What 24h > Architecture is doing in Thailand, on a promontory a few steps from an extremely beautiful beach, is dream architecture, combining a strong iconic impact with great refinement in construction, and this using local materials and techniques. The pavilion provides a home for activities for children, and includes an auditorium, library and rooms equipped for play and reading. The form of the structure is inspired by a manta that in this case seems to fly over the vegetation like a large fish sailing over the weeds. The roof, which in some points is 8 metres high, comprises a mass of bamboo whose floral jumble recalls some baroque decoration. The interior adds another local timber to the bamboo, River Red Gum Wood, which is a type of eucalyptus used in the past by Australian Aborigines.

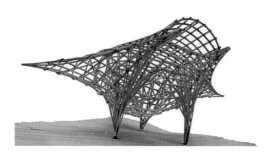

Atelier Oslo
AWP

The Lantern

2008
Sandnes, Norway

The town of Sandnes in Norway required the construction of a shelter in a square in the town centre. The designers (a team of Norwegians and French) started with the idea of creating an object with a strong iconic value, able to hold a dialogue directly with the citizens. They thus decided to use the schematic silhouette of a local house and to suspend it over the square. The project consists of a superimposition of three elements: wooden stylized tree-shaped columns, a structural coffered ceiling, also of wood, and a transparent envelope around the whole. By night, this suspended memory of the rural world made a public space is lit up like a lantern.

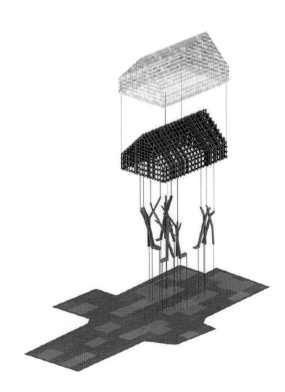

Álvaro Siza Vieira
Eduardo Souto de Moura
Cecil Balmond

Serpentine Gallery Pavilion

2005
London, United
Kingdom

The image of this temporary pavilion is that of an archaic Berber tent reinterpreted in wood. To give it its form, the architects adopted a grid that deforms like a tent; this grid was made from elements of wood blocked together using simple technology but in accordance with a complex design. A fundamental role in the design and construction of this solid tent was played by structural designer Cecil Balmond, who had already worked with Siza in the Portuguese Pavilion at the Universal Expo of Lisbon. The grid is panelled with polycarbonate sheets that do not reach as far down as the ground and so give the tent a sensation of floating above the earth.

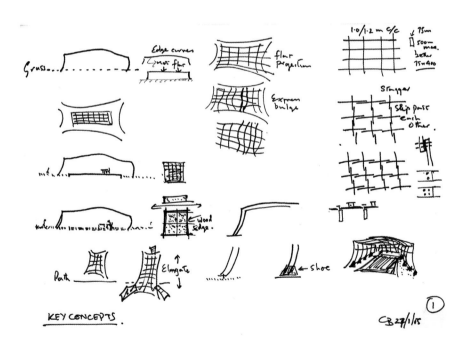

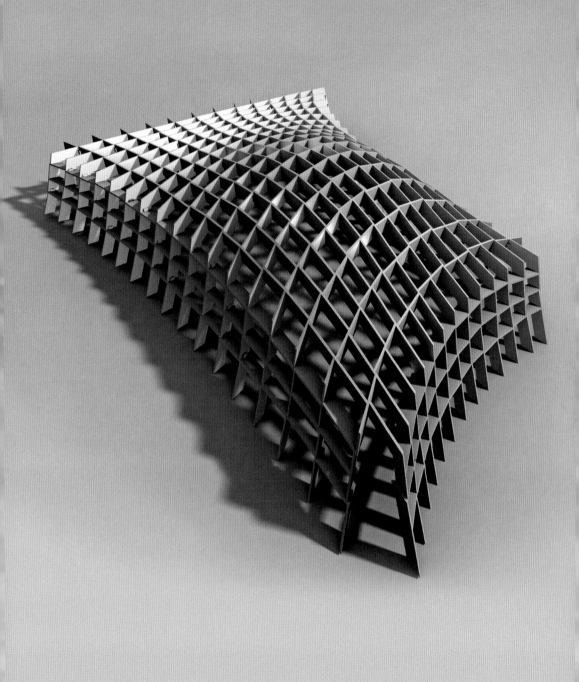

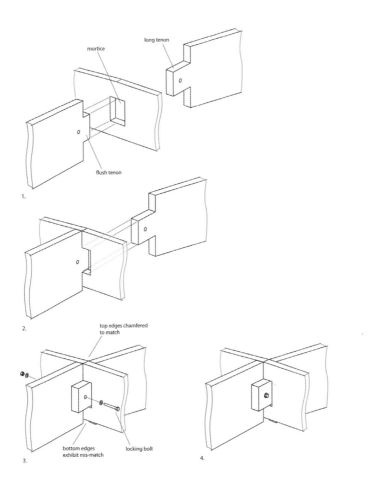

1.

mortice

long tenon

flush tenon

2.

3.

top edges chamfered
to match

bottom edges
exhibit mis-match

locking bolt

4.

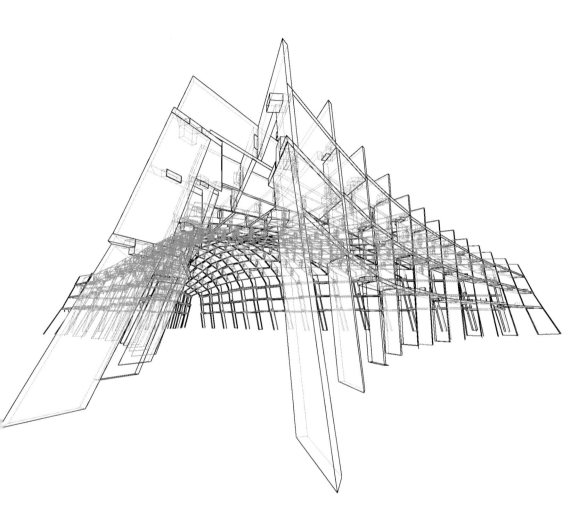

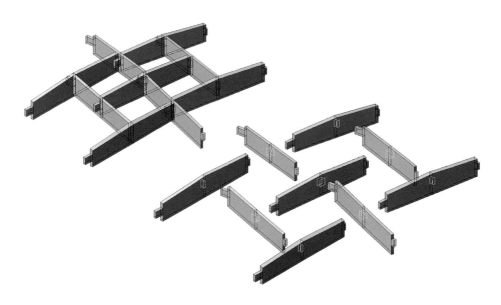

Frank O. Gehry   **Serpentine Gallery Pavilion**

2008
London, United
Kingdom

In this project, Gehry abandons the envelopes that have made him famous
to return to his origins, when he used to propose an architecture of exploded
fragments in Los Angeles in the seventies, most of the time made using recycled
components, joined together to mimic an explosion. The pavilion in London
aims to be a mix of public square, promenade and room, and may overall
be considered a theatrical machine to be lived as aesthetic experience. Speaking
of the pavilion, Gehry declares he was inspired by Leonardo da Vinci's machines,
by their rational and enigmatic appeal.

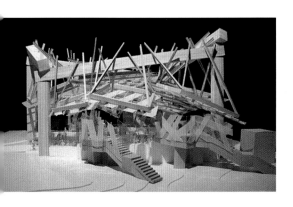

Bruder Klaus Chapel

2007
Mechernich, Germany

The chapel is an ex-voto desired by the owners of the land. Despite its simplicity, the tiny church reveals a complex story. Zumthor wanted an involvement of the clients, who cut the 111 trees needed as formwork for the concrete casting shaping the upper part of the chapel, which is 12 metres high. The casting was effected over 24 days so as to cast 50 cm a day. Zumthor has called this ritual technology "rammed concrete". After casting the concrete, fire was applied within so that the trunks burned away leaving a trace of their combustion on the cement.

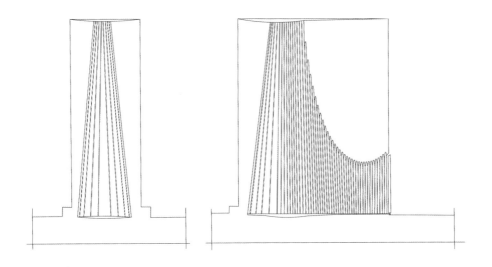

Rintala Eggertsson
Architects

Kaluga Floating Sauna

2008
Kaluga, Russia

As part of the *Objects for the Landscape* event held at Kaluga in Russia in 2008, Rintala Eggertsson built a sequence of four pavilions over the water of the river, to represent four primitive, essential forms of architecture. Overall, the project seems the *mise en scène* of de Quincy's idea who, in contrast to Laugier, saw not only the simple hut as one of the very earliest forms of architecture, but also the tent and the cave, all of which are archetypical forms that can be referred to a given culture.

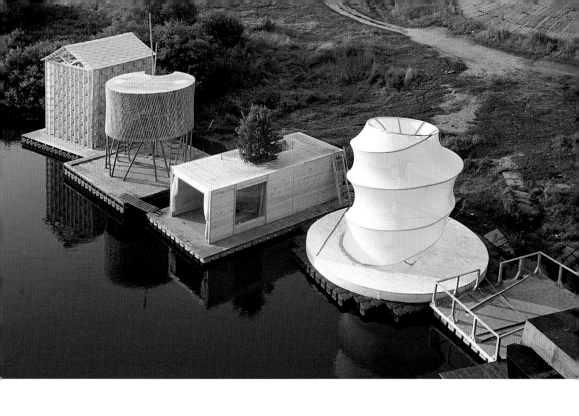

Edward Cullinan
Architects
Buro Happold

Downland Gridshell

1996–2002
Sussex, United
Kingdom

Cullinan Architects built what might be compared to an arch on the roof of a pavilion. The large roof has a double-curve geometry extending over 48 metres, with a maximum breadth of 16 metres and a maximum height of 10 metres. The structure is built from an overlay of four layers of a structural mesh formed of extremely slender (50 x 35 mm) rods of wood; the spacing between these rods varies from a maximum of 1 metre to 50 cm in the areas of greatest load. The structure was "woven" 7 metres above the ground on a provisional structure and then lowered, dismantling the supporting structure bit by bit. As soon as it was in its final position, the arch was made rigid with longitudinal and transversal beams.

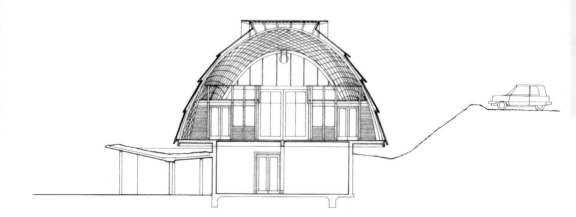

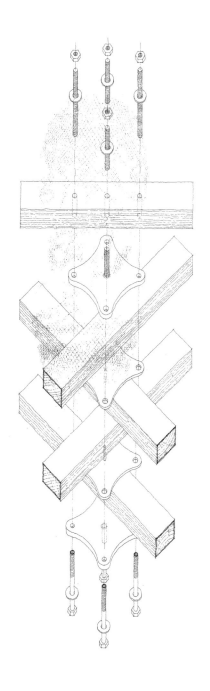

Nude and Naked

Hans Ibelings

Every category implies the existence of an opposing category. Thus, if there is a "naked" architecture, there must necessarily also be a "dressed" one.

Granted the existence of a naked architecture and of a dressed one, therefore, the question that arises is whether buildings are born naked (as the Dutch architect, Willem Jan Neutelings, affirms) or whether they have to be undressed to reveal their nakedness. In the selection Valerio Paolo Mosco proposes for his *Naked Architecture*, one has the impression that as far as the author is concerned, buildings are born naked and should remain so. His is a different stance, if not diametrically opposite, to that of Neutelings for whom buildings, born naked, should be dressed.

From an etymological point of view, the concept of nakedness involves being oneself completely, but the first impression one has of the works presented is that of buildings that are unfinished. The many views of building sites presented stress this sense of incompletion that remains even once the work is finished and the site closed. One could therefore affirm that Naked Architecture reduces the distance between building under construction and building finished to a minimum, to the point that it tends to correspond ideally with the act of building itself. In a final analysis, most of the buildings presented in the book, despite being built, suggest through their naked presence that they are still under construction. But what is under construction is not yet defined, and this condition suggests a sensation of openness that gives Naked Architecture a less dominant and conclusive presence than those buildings that borrow instead from Alberti's affirmation that beauty is a harmonious whole in which nothing can be added or removed without destroying the whole impression.

The character of openness, of unfinished, in many expressions of Naked Architecture is reflected in the "naked" text by Mosco, which is constructed carefully. The text offers an original, unexpected reading of contemporary architectural culture. One of the openings suggested by the text is the possibility of effecting a distinction between *nude* and *naked*. It seems to me that Mosco uses the two terms indiscriminately, probably because in Italian the distinction does not exist, but I believe that within the context of the architecture he presents, one could indeed see a difference between clearly *naked* architecture, which displays its intimate parts (in a "decent" or "indecent" manner), and one that is instead *nude*, where by *nude* I intend an aesthetic interpretation of the word, similar to that used in the history of art. If we adopt this distinction, the *nude* projects reveal an attraction for an atmospheric and tactile materialism, and this independently of what happens behind their exposed skin. On the basis of taste, therefore, we perceive this nudity with the same intensity that the less delicate, more deliberately nude projects emanate. So on the basis of a moral choice, some might, with regard to aesthetic or sensual nudity, prefer the deliberate display of a pure and innocent nudity. On the one hand, therefore, Lacaton and Vassal (*naked*), and on the other, Aires Mateus (*nude*).

One of the historical references indicated by Mosco for Naked Architecture is Hendrik Petrus Berlage, whose work has been defined by Manfred Bock, one of the most authoritative experts on Berlage, as being of a "stubborn beauty". Bock's comment is a polite way of saying that honesty and frankness are not actually that elegant. Let us return to the distinction: *nude* architecture is elegant and refined, while *naked* architecture prefers to show things as they are, however inopportune or disreputable this may be. *Nude* architecture aims to offer an impression, therefore, while its *naked* counterpart is unable to pretend, given that it is by nature honest and in most cases tends towards innocence.

Without Valerio Paolo Mosco, I would never have made this crucial distinction by which *Nude Architecture* concerns beauty, while *Naked Architecture* concerns honesty. From a rational point of view, it should be simpler to appreciate honesty, while from an emotional one, instead, it is hard not to be seduced by beauty. In an ideal situation, beauty and honesty go together. In life, in art and in architecture.

Bibliography

About the idea of nakedness

Agamben, Giorgio, *Nudities* (Palo Alto: Stanford University Press, 2010).

Ariemma, Tommaso, *Il senso del nudo* (Milan: Mimesis Edizioni, 2008).

Bacon, Francis, *Interviews with Francis Bacon: The Brutality of Fact* (London: Thames & Hudson, 1981).

Barcan, Ruth, *Nudity: a Cultural Anatomy (Dress, Body, Culture)* (London: Berg Publisher, 2004).

Barthes, Roland, *Writing Degree Zero* (New York: Hill and Wang, 1968) [*Le degré zéro de l'écriture* (Paris: Éditions du Seuil, 1953)].

Baudelaire, Charles, *The Painter of Modern Life and Other Essays* (London: Phaidon Press, 2006) [*Le Peintre de la Vie Moderne* (Paris: 1863); *L'Art Romantique* (Paris: 1863)].

Baudelaire, Charles, *My Heart Laid Bare* (New York: Mal-O-Mar, 2009).

Benjamin, Walter, *Angelus Novus* (Berlin: Suhrkamp Verlag, 1988).

Bortoft, Henry, *The Wholeness of Nature: Goethe's Way Toward Science of Conscious Participation in Nature* (Great Barrington: Lindisfarne Books, 1996).

Carr-Gomm, Philip, *A Brief History of Nakedness* (London: Reaktion Book, 2010).

Cassirer, Ernst, *Philosophy of Symbolic Forms*, vol.1-2-3 (New Heaven: Yale University Press, 1965) [*Zur Metaphysik der symbolischen Formen* (Hamburg: 1920)].

Chimirri, Giovanni, *Psicologia della nudità: l'etica del pudore fra esibizione e intimità* (Pavia: Bonomi editore, 2010).

Critique D'Art: Charles Baudelaire, Denis Diderot, Theophile Gautier, Joris-Karl Huysmans, Yves Bonnefoy, Malcolm de Chazal, Paul Adam, edited by Livres Groupes (New York: Barnes & Noble, 2010).

Cunningham, Jim, *Nudity & Christianity,* (Indiana: Author House, 2006).

Desideri, Fabrizio, Cantelli, Chiara, *Storia dell'estetica occidentale: da Omero alle neuroscienze* (Rome: Carocci, 2008).

Eliade, Mircea, *The Sacred and the Profane* (New York: Harcourt, Brace & World, 1959) [*Briser le toit de la maison* (Paris: Gallimard, 1986)].

Goethe's Way of Science (Environmental and Architectural Phenomenology), edited by David Seamon, Arthur Zajonc (New York: Suny, 1998).

Hegel, Georg Wilhelm Friedrich, Knox T. M., *Hegel's Aesthetics; Lectures on Fine Arts* (London: Oxford University Press, 1975) [*Vorlesungen über die Ästhetik*, Berlin-Weimar 1835–38].

Leslie, Esther, *Walter Benjamin* (London: Reaktion Book, 2007).

Nancy, Jean-Luc, *Corpus* (New York: Fordham University Press, 2008).

Nancy, Jean-Luc, *Noli Me Tangere: On the Raising of the Body* (New York: Fordham University Press, 2008).

O'Reilly, Sally, *The Body in Contemporary Art* (London: Thames and Hudson, 2009).

Paz, Octavio, *Marcel Duchamp: Appearance Stripped Bare* (New York: Viking Press, 1978) [*Apariencia desnuda*, Mexico City: Era, 1966].

Plato, "Charmides", in *Plato: Charmides, Alcibiades 1&2, Hipparchus, The Lovers...* (Cambridge, MA: Loeb Classical Library, 1927).

Rella, Franco, *Ai confini del corpo* (Milan: Feltrinelli, 2000).

Sartre, Jean-Paul, *Being and Nothingness: an Essay in Phenomenological Ontology* (New York: Citadel Press, 1956) [*L'Être et le néant: Essai d'ontologie phénoménologique* (Paris: Gallimard, 1943)].

Sedlmayr, Hans, *Art in Crisis: The Lost Center* (Piscataway, New Jersey: Transaction Publishers, 2006) [*Verlust der Mitte* (Salzburg: Otto Müller Verlag, 1948)].

Simmel, Georg,
"The Ruin", in *Georg
Simmel, 1858–1919:
A Collection of Essays*,
ed. and trans. by Kurt
Wolff (Columbus: Ohio
State University Press,
1959), pp. 259–66.

Simpson, David, *German
Aesthetic and Literary
Criticism: Kant, Fichte,
Schelling, Schopenhauer,
Hegel* (Cambridge: Press
Syndacate University
of Cambridge, 1984).

Vettese, Angela, "Il corpo
inquieto", in *Capire l'arte
contemporanea* (Turin:
Allemandi, 2006).

Zajonc, Arthur G., *Facts
as Theory: Aspects
of Goethe's Philosophy
of Science* (Boston:
Reidel Publishing Comp.,
1987).

About nakedness
in architecture

Banham, Reyner, *Theory
and Design in the first
Machine Age* (London:
Architectural Press,
1960).

Banham, Reyner,
*New Brutalism: Ethic
or Aesthetic* (London:
Reinhold Publishing
Corporation, 1966).

Banham, Reyner,
*A Concrete Atlantis U.S.
Industrial Building and
European Modern
Architecture 1900–1925*,
(Cambridge, MA:
The MIT Press, 1986).

Banham, Reyner,
*Architettura della seconda
età della macchina*,
edited by Marco Biraghi
(Milan: Electa, 2004).

Berlage, Hendrik Petrus,
*Gedanken über Stil in der
Bukunst* (Leipzig: Julius
Zeitler, 1905).

Cacciari, Massimo,
*Architecture and Nihilism:
On the Philosophy
of Modern Architecture*
(New Haven: Yale
University Press, 1993).

Collins, Peter, *Concrete:
The Vision of a New
Architecture. A Study
of Auguste Perret and his
Precursors* (London-New
York: Faber & Faber,
1959).

Dal Co, Francesco,
*Figures of Architecture
and Thought: German
Architecture Culture
1880-1920* (New York:
Rizzoli International,
1990).

Dirindin, Riccardo,
*Lo stile dell'ingegneria.
Architettura e identità
della tecnica tra il primo
modernismo e Pier Luigi
Nervi* (Venice: Marsilio,
2010).

Elliot, Cecile D., *Technics
and Architecture:
The Development of
Materials and Systems
for Buildings* (Cambridge,
MA: The MIT Press,
1992).

Fanelli, Giovanni,
Gargiani, Roberto, *Il
principio del rivestimento:
prolegomena a una storia
dell'architettura
contemporanea*
(Rome-Bari: Laterza,
1994).

Fanelli, Giovanni,
Gargiani, Roberto, *Storia
dell'architettura
contemporanea: spazio,
struttura, involucro*
(Rome-Bari: Laterza,
1998 (2004²).

Forty, Adrian, *Words
and Buildings: a
Vocabulary of Modern
Architecture* (London:
Thames & Hudson,
2000).

Frampton, Kenneth,
*Studies on Tectonic
Culture: The Poetics
of Construction
in Nineteenth and
Twentieth Century
Architecture* (Cambridge,
MA: The MIT Press,
1995).

Gargiani, Roberto,
*Teoria e opere di Auguste
Perret 1874–1954*
(Milan: Electa, 1993).

Giedion, Siegfried,
Space, Time, Architecture
(Cambridge, MA: Harvard
University Press, 1941).

Giedion, Siegfried,
The Eternal Present
(London: Oxford
University Press, 1962).

Gravagnuolo, Benedetto,
*Gottfried Semper.
Architettura, arte
e scienza. Scritti scelti.
1834–1869* (Neaples:
Clean, 1987).

Herrmann, Wolfgang,
*Gottfried Semper:
In search of Architecture*
(Cambridge, MA:
The MIT Press, 1984).

Herrmann, Wolfgang,
*Laugier and Eighteenth-
Century French Theory*
(London: Zwemmer,
1962).

Hübsh, Heinrich, *In What Style Should We Build? The German Debate on Architectural Style* (Santa Monica: Getty Center for the History of Art and Humanities, 1991) [*In Welchem Stil sollen wir bauen?* (Karlsruhe: 1828)].

Kahn, Louis I., "Building Engineering", in *Architectural Forum*, November 1952, pp. 148–52.

Kahn, Louis I., "Monumentality", in *Architecture, You and Me: The Diary of a Development* (Cambridge, MA: Harvard University Press, 1958).

Kaufmann, Emil, *Architecture in the Age of Reason. Baroque and Post-Baroque in England, Italy and France* (Cambridge, MA: Harvard University Press, 1955).

Laugier, Marc-Antoine, *Essay on Architecture* (Los Angeles: Hennessey & Ingalls Inc., 1977) [*Essai sur l'architecture* (Paris: 1753)].

Le Corbusier, *Towards a New Architecture* (London: John Rodker, 1931) [*Vers une architecture* (Paris: Édition Crés, 1923)].

Loos, Adolf, *Spoken into the Void: Collected Essays 1897–1900* (Cambridge, MA: The MIT Press, 1982) [*Ins Leere gesprochen. Aufsätze im Wiener Zeitungen und Zeitschriften aus den Jahren 1897–1900* (Paris: Édition Crés, 1921)].

Mallgrave, Harry Francis, *Gottfried Semper: The Four Elements of Architecture and Other Writings* (New York: Cambridge University Press, 1989).

Mallgrave, Harry Francis (with Eleftherios Ikonomou), *Empathy, Form, and Space: Problems in German Aesthetics 1873–1893* (Santa Monica: Getty Publication Programs, 1994).

Mallgrave, Harry Francis, *Modern Architectural Theory 1673–1968* (New York: Cambridge University Press, 2005).

Mallgrave, Harry Francis (with David Goodman), *An Introduction to Architectural Theory: 1968 to the Present* (Hoboken: Wiley-Blackwell Press, 2010).

Masiero, Roberto, *Estetica dell'architettura* (Bologna: Il Mulino, 1999).

Milizia, Francesco, *Dell'arte di vedere nelle belle arti e nel disegno* (Venice: 1781; Pistoia: Tariffi, 1944).

Moussavi, Farshid, Kubo, Michael, *The Function of Ornament* (Barcelona-Cambridge, MA: Actar-Harvard University Press, 2007).

Moussavi, Farshid, Kubo, Michael, *The Function of Form* (Barcelona-Cambridge, MA: Actar-Harvard University Press, 2009).

Neumeyer, Fritz, *The Artless Word. Mies van der Rohe on the Building Art* (Cambridge, MA: The MIT Press, 1991) [*Mies van der Rohe. Das kunstlose Wort. Gedanken zur Baukunst* (Berlin: Wolf Jobst Siedler GmbH, 1986)].

Norberg-Shulz, Christian, *Principles of Modern Architecture* (London: Andreas Papadakis Publishers, 2000).

Pevsner, Nikolaus, *Pioneers of Modern Design: from William Morris to Walter Gropius* (New Heaven: Yale University Press, 1943).

Polano, Sergio, *Hendrik Petrus Berlage. Opera Completa* (Milan: Electa, 1999).

Riegl, Alois, *Problems of Style* (Princeton: Princeton University Press, 1992) [*Stilfragen* (Berlin: 1893)].

Rowe, Colin, *The Mathematics of the Ideal Villa and other Essays* (Cambridge, MA: The MIT Press, 1976).

Rowe, Colin, *The Architecture of Good Intentions* (London: Academy Editions, 1994).

Rykwert Joseph, *The First Moderns: The Architects of the Eighteenth Century* (Cambridge, MA: The MIT Press, 1980).

Rykwert, Joseph, *The Necessity of Artifice: Ideas in Architecture* (New York-London: Rizzoli International, 1982).

Scully, Vincent jr., *Louis Kahn* (New-York- London, George Braziller Inc., 1963).

Scully, Vincent jr., "Louis I. Kahn and the Ruins of Rome", in Id., *Modern Architecture and Other Essays*, edited by Neil Levine (Princeton: Princeton University Press, 2003), p. 311.

Semper, Gottfried,
*The Four Elements of
Architecture and Other
Writings,* edited by Harry
Francis Mallgrave,
Wolfgang Herrmann
(Cambridge, MA:
Cambridge University
Press, 1991) [*Die vier
Elemente der Baukunst.
Ein Beitrag zur
vergleichenden Baukunde*
(Braunschweig: Verlag
Friederich Vieweg
und Sohn, 1852)].

Semper, Gottfried,
*Lo Stile nelle arti tecniche
e tettoniche o estetica
pratica. Manuale per
tecnici, artisti e amatori*
(Rome-Bari, Laterza,
1992) [*Der Stil in den
technishen und
tektonishen Künsten oder
praktishe Ästhetik. Ein
Handbuch für Techniker,
Künstler und
Kunstfreunde,* vol. 1,
(Frankfurt: 1860)].

Solà-Morales, Ignasi de,
*Archeologia del Moderno.
Da Durand a Le Corbusier*
(Turin: Allemandi, 2005).

Venturi, Robert,
*Complexity and
Contradiction in
architecture* (New York:
The Museum of Modern
Art, 1966).

Viollet-le-Duc, Eugène,
*The Habitations of Man
in All Ages* (London:
1876) [*Histoire de
l'habitation humaine*
(Paris: 1875)].

Wagner, Otto, *Modern
Architecture: a Guidebook
for His Students to This
Field of Art,* edited by
Harry Mallgrave (Santa
Monica: Getty Center
for the History of Art and
the Humanities, 1988)
[*Moderne Architektur.
Seinen Schülern ein
Führer auf diesem
Kunstgebiete* (Vienna:
Schroll, 1895)].

Zevi, Bruno, *Architettura
in nuce* (Venice-Rome:
Istituto per la
Collaborazione Culturale,
1960).

Zevi, Bruno, "Il grado
zero della scrittura
architettonica",
in *Pretesti di critica
architettonica*
(Turin: Einaudi, 1983),
pp. 273-279.

**About the idea
of structural nudity
and the idea of frugal
nudity**

Abbate, Cinzia, Spina,
Maria, Zevi, Adachiara,
*Per una architettura
frugale / Toward a Frugal
Architecture* (Rome:
Fondazione Bruno Zevi,
2010).

A+U: Cecil Balmond,
Japan, November 2006.

Balmond, Cecil, *Informal:
The Informal in
Architecture and in
Engineering* (London:
Prestel, 2002).

Brandi, Cesare,
Struttura e Architettura
(Turin: Einaudi, 1975).

Conzett, Jürg, Mostafavi,
Mohsen, *Structure
as Space: Engineering
and Architecture in the
Works of Jürg Conzett*
(London: Architectural
Association, 2006).

Cruvellier, Mark R., Eggen
P. Arne, Sandaker, Bjorn
N., *The Structural Basis
of Architecture*
(London-New York:
Routledge, 2011).

Douglis, Evan,
Autogenetic Structures
(New York: Taylor
and Francis, 2009).

Fathy, Hassan,
*Architecture for the Poor.
An Experiment in Rural
Egypt* (Chicago:
University of Chicago
Press, 1973).

Fehn, Sverre,
"Archaic Modernism",
in *Architectural Review,*
no. 1071, May 1986,
pp. 57–60.

*Giuseppe Pagano
fotografo,* edited
by Cesare de Seta
(Milan: Electa, 1979).

Hall, Sir James Bart,
*On the Origins and
Principles of Gothic
Architecture* (London:
1813).

Margolius, Ivan,
*Architects + Engineers =
Structures* (London:
Wiley Academy, 2002).

*Nervi: Space and
Structural Integrity,*
exhibition catalogue
(San Francisco:
San Francisco Museum
of Modern Art, 1961).

Nordenson, Guy, Riley,
Terence, *Seven Structural
Engineers: the Felix
Candela Lecture*
(New York: The Museum
of Modern Art, 2008).

Rice, Peter, *An Engineer
Images* (London: Artemis,
1993).

Rykwert, Joseph, *On Adam's House in Paradise: The Idea of Primitive Hut in Architectural History* (Cambridge, MA: The MIT Press, 1972).

Rudofsky, Bernard, *Architecture without Architects: a Short Introduction to non-pedigreed Architecture,* exhibition catalogue (New York: Museum of Modern Art, 1965).

Sabatino, Michelangelo, *Pride in Modesty: Modernist: Architecture and the Vernacular Tradition in Italy* (Toronto: University of Toronto Press, 2010).

Saint, Andrew, *Architects and Engineers: a Study in Sibling Rivalry* (New Haven-London: Yale University Press, 2007).

Sasaki, Mutsuro, *Flux Structure* (Tokyo: Toto Edition, 2005).

Tessenow, Heinrich, *Hausbau und dergleichen* (Berlin: Woldemar Klein Verlag, 1916).

"The New Structuralism: Design, Engineering and Architectural Technologies", in *AD*, no. 4, 2010, guest editors Oxman Rivka, Oxman Robert.

Wells, Matthew, *Engineers: a Story of Engineering and Structural Design* (New York: Routledge, 2010).

Credits